The Four Competitive Business Drivers

Theory, Model, Strategy, Tactics

The Four Competitive Business Drivers

Theory, Model, Strategy, Tactics

Jorge Sá
Magda Pereira

BEP
BUSINESS EXPERT PRESS
Leader in applied, concise business books

The Four Competitive Business Drivers:
Theory, Model, Strategy, Tactics

Cover design by Célia César.

Interior design by S4Carlisle Publishing Services, Chennai, India

First published in 2025 by
Business Expert Press, LLC
222 East 46th Street, New York, NY 10017
www.businessexpertpress.com

ISBN-13: 978-1-63742-916-7 (paperback)
ISBN-13: 978-1-63742-917-4 (e-book)

Strategic Management Collection

First edition: 2025

10 9 8 7 6 5 4 3 2 1

EU SAFETY REPRESENTATIVE
Mare Nostrum Group B.V.
Mauritskade 21D
1091 GC Amsterdam
The Netherlands
gpsr@mare-nostrum.co.uk

Acknowledgments

This book would not have been possible without the continuous support and major contributions of many, most specially of the managing editor Scott Isenberg, Professor Jack Pearce, Charlene Kronstedt, Gajalakshmi Sivakumar, among others.

To all our gratitude. Naturally that any shortcomings are the sole responsibility of the authors.

Dedication

To Teresa and Mário.

Description

Management books frequently make a clear-cut distinction between **strategy** and **tactics**.

Seldom, however, do they include the **business model** as a *third* competitiveness driver distinct from the former two.

And never so far has the **theory of business** been considered as a *fourth* required performance vector, different from all the other three: indeed frequently it is blurred with the business model.

However, organizational optimization requires that all four interact since they all are **necessary** conditions for organization optimization: the *why*, *where*, *what*, and *how*.

The **theory of business** (first introduced by Peter Drucker in the 1990s) is the *why* the company makes sense. The reality assumptions the organization is grounded upon. What it is paid for.

The **business model** (popularized by Michael Porter and others in the early 2000s) is the *what*: the basic pillars, the stepping stones of a firm's organization. How it transforms clients' satisfaction into value for itself.

Then both the theory of business (*why*) and the business model (*what*) are distinct from **strategy**, which is (according to Joffre) the *where*: the choice of (1) geographical areas, (2) industries, and (3) (within them of) segments.

Finally, the fourth competitiveness driver is **tactics**—the *how*—and which respects to the nine functional areas, from marketing (as per Philip

Kotler) to human resources to finance and so on: how to advertise, how to motivate, how to finance operations, how....

From the above model follows several inferences.

First, all four drivers are *necessary* conditions, none by itself is sufficient. That means that excellence is required in all for performance optimization and (at the very least) satisfactory execution for organization survival.

Second, they are *interrelated*, some impacting on the others.

Third (and consequently), they must make sense all together. Their mix must *reinforce* each other. Be compatible. There must be a fit.

Fourth, they should be periodically *reviewed*. Due to environmental changes (e.g., Sears Roebuck), benchmark innovations (Spotify versus Apple Music) or the business model slowly drifting away step by step (as in the case of Marks & Spencer).

And *finally*, there are a sequence of *steps* which—if followed—will simplify the revision of all four competitiveness drivers and how they best fit together.

That is what is illustrated by the book's **examples**, analyzed in great detail: for example, Nike, Dollar Shave Club, SpaceX, Scholl, Gerber, Vendôme, Spotify, Sears Roebuck, IBM, ATT, Apple Music, McDonald's, Marks & Spencer, Canva, SolarCity, Tesla, Better Place, Gorillas, Getir, Farfetch, to name a few.

The **overall message** is that neglect of any of the four competitiveness drivers will mean ever-greater *efficiency* (*doing things right—the Phronesis of Aristotle*), but ever-lower *effectiveness* (*doing the right things—the Chokhmah of Solomon*).

With the consequence of underperformance. Because actions will be **off target**. More and more resources are devoted to producing less and less.

Contents

Chapter 1   **Introduction:** How the Four Competitiveness
             Drivers Are **Distinct**..1

Chapter 2   **Theory of Business:** How **Nike** Overtook *Adidas;*
             Dollar Shave Club Outperformed *Gillette;*
             and **SpaceX** Came to Dominate the Space *Industry* 7

Chapter 3   **Business Model:** Why It Took **Nearly Two Decades**
             for **Spotify** to Achieve **Profitability** (While **SolarCity**
             Revolutionized Its Industry from **the Start**) 45

Chapter 4   *Why, How,* and *When* to **Review** the
             Theory of Business 75

Chapter 5   *Why, When,* and *How* to **Review** the
             Business Model 99

Chapter 6   **Conclusion:** The **Four Drivers** (*Business Theory* +
             Business Model + *Strategy* + *Tactics*) as **Prerequisites**
             for Competitiveness..123

Selected References...155

About the Authors...159

Index 163

CHAPTER 1

Introduction: How the Four Competitiveness Drivers Are Distinct

There is nothing as practical as a good theory.
(Kurt Lewin)

The theory of business was introduced by *Peter Drucker* in the 1990s.[1]

Then the concept of **business model** was popularized by *Michael Porter* and others in the beginning of the millennium.[2]

And in the following decades they have been used *indistinctively*, although they are quite different concepts.

The **theory of business** is the *reality assumptions* a company is grounded upon. **Why it makes sense**. What the company is *paid for* (as Peter Drucker put it).

And the **business model** is the basic *pillars,* the stepping stones, of a firm's *organization*. How it *transforms* clients satisfaction into *value* for itself. *Profits*.

And then both business theory and business model are also **distinct** from **strategy**, a concept imported from the military and which refers to *where* to compete (the choice of geographical areas, industries, and segments), and from **tactics**, the *how* of functional areas: marketing, finance, operations, and so on (how to promote, how to finance, how to organize production, how...).[3]

Organizational optimization requires first of all a sound *theory of business* (the hypothesis on what the company has been built upon—**why** it makes sense). Then to define well both its *strategy* (the **where**—the areas of activity) and the *business model* (**what** are the basic functions, pillars of the organization). And, finally, the *tactical plans*: the **how** from marketing to budgeting.

---

[1]Drucker (1994).

[2]Although the term was first used by Bellman in 1957, it came into prominence after an article by Porter (2001).

[3]There are nine functional, tactical areas: (1) marketing, (2) human resources, (3) finance, (4) accounting, (5) operations, (6) R&D, (7) information systems, (8) administrative (maintenance, security, hygiene, catering, etc.), and (9) general management (organization chart, control and coordination mechanisms).

All together they constitute the **four drivers for competitiveness**: the *why*, *what*, *where*, and *how* to compete (Figure 1).

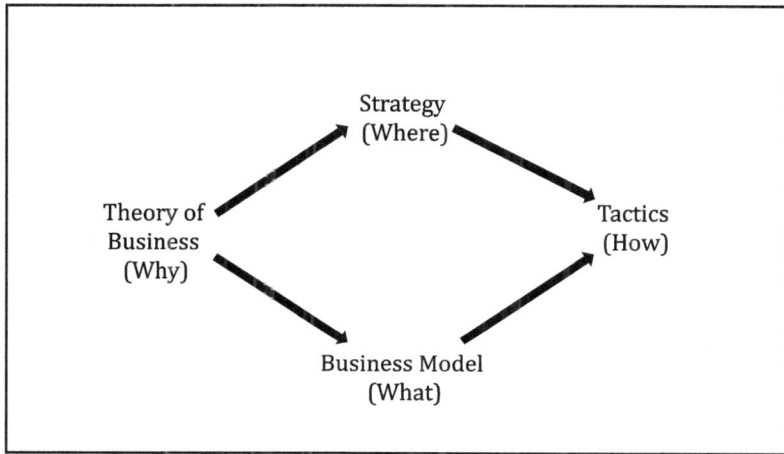

Figure 1 The four competitiveness drivers

Besides distinct, competitiveness requires that all four (1) *fit to* reinforce each other, (2) be *periodically reviewed* to update them to environment changes, and (3) in a *preset sequence of steps*.

That is the **basic message** of this book which is organized as follows.

The next chapter makes the case for the importance of the *theory of business* with the examples of Nike against Adidas and Puma. Then of Dollar Shave Club overtaking Gillette and Schick. And, finally, SpaceX further illustrates how the theory of business can be a source of differentiation and, consequently, of success.

The following chapter focuses on the *business model* and its impact exemplified by the cases of SolarCity, McDonald's, and Spotify, that, in spite of having by far always the largest market share, failed to produce profits for almost two decades after its inception in 2006 (by opposition to competitors such as Apple Music).[4]

---

[4]Spotify reached profitability only in its 19th year (2024) of operations, due to changes performed on its business model as analyzed in Chapter 3.

Thus, there is a need to periodically review **both** the theory of business and the business model. How to go about that and when is analyzed in Chapters 4 and 5.

The last chapter illustrates how the above two tasks are **distinct** from (periodically) checking on *strategy* and *tactics* with the examples of Marks & Spencer, Tesla, Spotify, Farfetch, Getir, and Warby Parker.

All the above makes this a practical book. It stresses that there are **four separate drivers** for performance. And how to test all the four periodically.

And that **all four** are **necessary** conditions, none by itself is *sufficient*, for high competitiveness.

The penalty for failing to distinguish among them is off-target actions: increasing efforts to improve the unnecessary.[5]

And thus falling into the trap of doing things ever better, which, however, are simply not the right things to do—and so more resources producing ever less.

Let's start by distinguishing between the *theory of business* and the *business model*. And then both from *strategy* and *tactics*.

---

[5]Several recent works recognize the confusion among the concepts. For instance, the work by Peric et al. (2017), in Bigelow and Barney (2021) and Ademi et al. (2021).

Appendix

Together with the four competitiveness drivers of Figure 1 in Page 3, there is a related concept: the **mission**, the **business a company is in**.

Examples of mission definitions are, for example, for *Scholl*: *foot comfort* and, thus, it supplies on top of very comfortable shoes, special sandals, plasters, powders, and lotions all for clients suffering from several types of feet aches.

Gerber's mission is *babies are our business* and, therefore, it offers toys, lotions, shampoos, talcum powder, nappies, food, and so on.

Vendôme? We are in the luxury business (jewelry, pens, watches, etc.).

And so on.

Thus, at the **core** of the sentence defining an organization's mission, the business it is in, are the **needs**, the problems to be solved.

And those needs are not only a **direct consequence** but also an **integrant part** of (the reality assumptions of) the theory of business. *They are the fundamental problem that requires a solution.* For instance, in the case of *Nike*—to be analyzed next—the market was not supplying good-enough specialized shoes for runners (both on- and off-track).

So, in scheme:

Theory of business (Reality assumptions)	⟶	**Needs** (Mission/business the company is in: problem to be solved	⟶	**Business model** (How to get the job done)

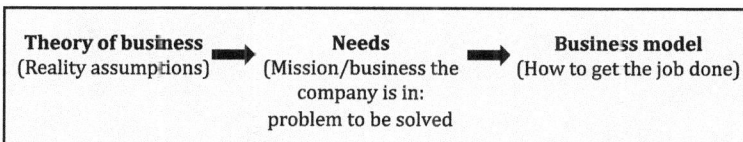

Thus, some companies find it useful to define their mission/the business they are in, in order to provide all with an idea of what they are in the market for (e.g., in the case of the *Salvation Army*: to make citizens out of the dejected; or the *American Girl*: We are in the little girl business).

But, since the **mission** is a sentence that makes explicit the **needs** that are a part of the **theory of business**, it is not worthwhile to make the mission stand alone in the model of Figure 1 in Page 3.

Anyway, those interested in pursuing further the topic of what is my business/mission and what should it be may find useful to check:

- *The first book* which ever addressed the topic: *Management*, by Peter Drucker in the 1973 edition (Chapters 5–7), Harper & Row; then
- A small and highly useful book—again by Peter Drucker— *The Five Most Important Questions You Will Ever Ask About Your Organization* (Chapter 1 with Jim Collins), Jossey-Bass, 2008; and
- A further detailed discussion of the topic can be found on the book by Jorge Vasconcellos e Sá and Magda Pereira: *Drucker on Carving Success Out of the Crisis: What Peter Drucker Would Have Told Us* (Chapter 5), Vida Económica, 2009.

CHAPTER 2

Theory of Business: How Nike Overtook *Adidas*; Dollar Shave Club Outperformed *Gillette*; and SpaceX Came to Dominate the Space *Industry*

Vision is the art of seeing what is invisible to others.
(Jonathan Swift)

2.1. Introduction

At the start, there is the **business plan:** *how a company plans to make money.*

That requires two things: *Phronesis* and *Chokhmah.*

Phronesis for *Aristotle* is the ability of linking means to ends.

And that refers to how to do it. **Efficiency.** *To do things right.*

It is the realm of operations functioning, of doing the same in a better, different, way—with downsizing, lean manufacturing, outsourcing, economic value analysis, benchmarking, reengineering, and so on.

Here, one deals with both:

- The **business model: What** are the fundamental pillars of the company functioning; and
- **The tactics**, the **functional** areas: **how** to recruit, motivate, control, and so on (Table 1).

Then there is the *Chokhmah*, which *Solomon* prayed for, namely, the capacity of selecting worthwhile objectives.

That regards what to do—**Effectiveness**—*to do the right things.*

And that refers also to the two variables shown in Table 1:

- The **theory of business**—the reality assumptions the company is based upon: **Why** does it make sense? How do we create value for customers?
- The **strategy**—the choice of **where** to compete in terms of geographical areas, industries, and segments. United States, Canada, UK, Japan? Distribution (and not plastics or information technology or...)? And within distribution, supermarkets (but not

hypermarkets) and proximity/neighborhood stores (but not cash and carries)?

Thus, in Table 1 there is the *why* (business theory), the *where* (strategy), the *what* (business model), and the *how* (tactics).

The first two refers to **effectiveness**: doing the right things (Chokhmah). The last two refers to **efficiency**: doing things right (Phronesis).

Table 1 Distinguishing among the four competitiveness drivers

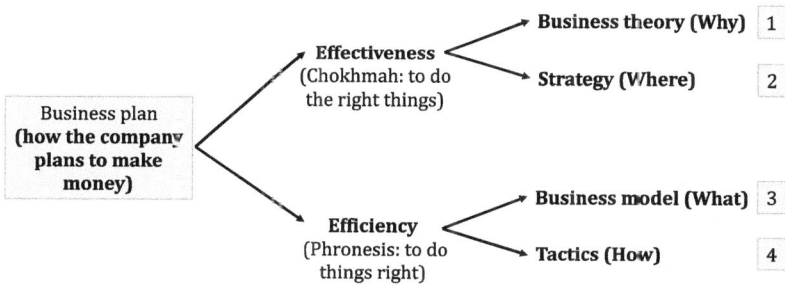

Competitiveness	Effectiveness (doing the right things)	Efficiency (doing things right)
Business theory	Why	
Strategy	Where	
Business model		What[6]
Tactics		How

A good **business plan** (*how to make money*) requires both **effectiveness** (doing the right things) and **efficiency** (doing things right). On its turn, effectiveness demands both sound theory of business (*why*) and strategy (*where*), whereas efficiency is achieved with the business model (*what*) and tactics (*how*).

---

[6]It can also be said that a business model respects to how a company operates. That is correct. However, since the focus is on the pillars, the stepping stones, the fundamentals, a business model is essentially a synthesis, a summary of operations. Thus, it is far better to define the **business model** as the **what** to distinguish it from the **how**, the detailed **tactics** of the several functional areas: human resources, marketing, finance, and so on.

Effectiveness (the *why* of business theory and *where* of strategy) is *external*.

Efficiency (the *what* of business model and *how* of tactics) is *internal*.

And *two further points* are noteworthy here.

First, a *frequent mistake* is whenever a company is underperforming, to jump at the immediate conclusion that the causes are internal—things such as bureaucracy, complacency, and incompetence.

However, in many cases, the true cause is external, starting with the hypotheses about a reality that do not hold true anymore. Their time has passed and they have become anachronisms.

Second, all four variables, including the theory of business and the business model, are always **controversial,** as they involve making **choices**. But, and as said, the theory of business requires to look outside, at the environment; in contrast, the business model is inwardly directed—its focus is on the inside.

A sound theory of business must fit reality and tap on **important facts, not trivia**. A good business model creates value for the organization while serving the customer.

Leaving for the next chapter the business model, let's analyze now in some detail the theory of business[7] with the help of three examples:

- Nike (against Adidas and Puma);
- Dollar Shave Club (facing Gillette and Schick); and finally
- SpaceX.

The latter two of the above examples illustrate how the theory of business remains highly important today as ever, in the digital age.

---

[7]As mentioned, the theory of business was first introduced in an article with such a title by Drucker (1994).

2.2. How Nike Overtook Adidas and Puma

2.2.1. The Theory of Business

When Nike was founded, **four** companies dominated the market: Adidas and Puma, and the smaller Reebok and Converse.

Nike was created by a partnership between Phil Knight (an accountant) and Bill Bowerman (an athletics coach). Neither of them was particularly wealthy.

However 16 years later, Nike had **50 percent** of the U.S. market share in all types of athletics shoes.

Nowadays (Figure 2), the market value of Nike is more than 5 times that of Adidas and 22 times that of Puma.

2023 World sports items market (in billion dollars)	Nike	Adidas	Puma
Sales	51,2	21,4	8,6
Market value	165,1	32,8	7,6

Figure 2 *Comparing Nike, Adidas, and Puma*

Source: Companies annual reports 2023; Statmuse.

Nike's sales top Adidas' by **140 percent** and by six times Puma's.[8]

How did *Nike* achieve such a *success*?

With **a novel theory of business** based on **five** assumptions (Table 2):

1. Racing (both off-track—joggers—and on-track—competition) was about to **boom**;
2. Racing required **specialized** shoes;
3. **There were no** good-enough specialized shoes;

---

[8]Both Reebok and Converse disappeared from the market as independent companies. The former was acquired by Adidas and the latter by Nike.

Table 2 Nike's theory of business (reality assumptions) at upstart (1964)

1	Running is about to **boom**	On-track (competition)
		Off-track (joggers)
2	Racing requires **specialized** shoes	
3	There is **no good-enough** specialized shoes	
4	Specialized shoes should have **five** characteristics	Light
		Comfortable
		Minimizing injuries
		Gripping power
		Outstanding design
5	It was possible to **undercut** market players' **prices** through Japanese imports	

4. Specialized shoes should have **five** characteristics:
   4.1. *As light* as possible;
   4.2. *Comfortable;*
   4.3. *Minimizing injuries;*
   4.4. With *gripping power;*
   4.5. An *appealing design*; and
5. It was possible with Japanese imports to **undercut the prices** of the dominant market players.

It is worthwhile to examine briefly how **novel** such a business theory was.

Until the arrival of Nike, the popularity of running (both on- and off-track) was far from established. In 1964 (at Nike's inception), the Boston Marathon had 403 participants. In 2024, that number rose to 30,000 (with the number of unaccepted applications far above).

Joggers were seen as a nuisance (people would shout and even throw objects at them), or even a pure illegal activity (with several cases of fines reported in cities across the United States). Joggers were seen as weirdos: What are they doing running on the streets? Are they crazy?

And consequently, both off- and on-track runners were a small niche compared to the far more popular sports such as American football, basketball, baseball, or ice hockey.

That means that Phil Knight did not notice an established booming trend. Instead, he noticed the upstart of a trend, at its very inception, beginning.

And so (in *Peter Drucker's* words), he was able to detect the future that had already happened; rather than a future trend, the futurity of a present trend, the part of the present pregnant with the future.

To jump into the trend meant staying ahead of the curve: If the Boston Marathon had less than 300 participants in 1963, a decade later in 1975 they were about 2,500 (more than eight times)—yearly growth of nearly 20 percent.

Then the **1970s** further intensified the exponential growth of runners.

It has been said that while in the 1960s people tried to change things (like racism and war) on a *social basis*, in the 1970s they worried about *themselves*: It was the *me* generation. The peacemakers of the 1960s were the joggers of the 1970s.

The first New York marathon in 1970 had 126 starters; in 1979, the field was limited to 14,000. Jim Fixx's 1977 "The Complete Book of Running" was 90 weeks in the *New York Times* bestseller list and two years later had sold 750,000 hardback copies.

There were **two reasons** for the drastic increase in jogging popularity. **First**, contrary to, for example, tennis, jogging numbers could *filter down* since it was *cheaper* and, thus, the average worker (the fireman, the postman, the secretary, the cabbies, the bank guards, whoever) could afford to run. **Second**, jogging is *quite practical*: It requires nothing and no one, making it the most democratic sport. One does not need a partner, a court, or even a skill. Only a t-shirt, shorts, sneakers, and off one goes.

Thus, a 1979 study (by Yankelovich, Skelly, and White Inc.) concluded that by the end of the 1970s decade, **one-sixth** of the U.S. population were runners.

And so it should come as no surprise that as demand grew so did competition and the variety of models: the special shoe edition of *Runner's*

World magazine in 1967 rated only 16 shoes, but in 1979 the number was already 178.

Then the **second, third,** and **fourth reality assumptions** (regarding the need for specialized shoes, its inexistence, and the must-have characteristics of sneakers [lines 2, 3, and 4 of Table 2]) came as much from cofounder B. Bowerman as it did from Phil Knight.

In 1964, generally brands did not make specialized shoes for jogging, although specialization mattered. *There were few specialized shoes in racing and those that existed were not good enough.*

Indeed, the 1966 ad of **Converse** (then one of the top four companies) differentiated only among (1) All Stars (basketball), (2) tennis, (3) track (both for indoors and outdoors for all kinds of sports, handball, volleyball, and so on, including racing), and (4) wrestling shoes (for boxing).

1966 ad of Converse (Source: eBay)

And brands such as Reebok that offered specialized shoes for racing were manufacturing spike shoes, that is, sneakers with spikes or cleats on the sole, made of metal or hard plastic, which while providing grip on the track surface, also created too much traction harming speed.

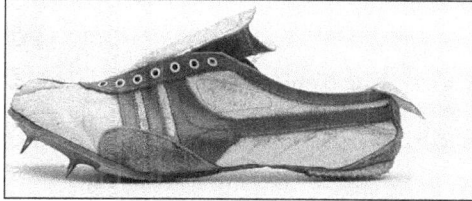

1961: A very early Reebok-made running spike featuring one of the first Reebok logos: the Olympic torch. (Source: www.ssense.com)

That they were unsatisfactory is demonstrated by the Canvas model ideal for racing introduced in 1966 by **Reebok**, two years after Nike's market entry in 1964. Gone were the spikes now replaced for lightness, which would henceforth be one of the distinctive features of racing shoes.

1966 ad of Reebok (Source: ret~obok.wordpress.com)

As Bowerman (racing coach and Phil Knight's partner) noted to start with, shoes should be as **light** as possible.[9] To run 1 mile (1.6 km), an average person with height of 6 feet (1.8 m) needs to make 880 steps. And so shoes weighing less than 1 ounce (0.028 kg), the amount per mile measures to less than 55 pounds (25 kg = 0.453 kg × 55).

Thus, at the time, Nike's idea was for sneakers to be as similar as possible to run with sockets or barefoot (and indeed many Kenyan athletes did so).

Comfort was from the start another must, since shoes are used for long uninterrupted periods (4 hours for men and 4.30 hours for women are considered excellent times in a marathon).

That was implemented with midsoles that were cushioned and slightly flexible to allow the feet to move and containing air, which enhanced comfort and decreased injuries.

Shoes should also make for **easy gripping** to avoid sliding, which, on top of being dangerous when running at high speed (especially in rainy weather or in cities sidewalks), made in competition for the loss of precious time needed to recuperate the balance.

As it happened, Bill Bowerman, while seeing his wife cooking waffles, had the idea of a waffle-type sole, making first the waffle of iron with urethane, then with plaster, and, finally, settling in stainless steel with punched roles plus liquid rubber, what was to become a tremendous success (Figure 3).

Finally, besides the characteristics of *light, comfortable,* and with *grip power,* the sneakers **design** should match the joggers personality: They choose a non-team sport since they are **individualists** who like to be **alone,** by themselves,—just a small step below rebels, which is the self-image of skaters.[10]

---

[9]Exemplifying that everything changes, nowadays the emphasis is not on lightness but impulse, and so the soles are high and made of various types of foams.
[10]There are several highly successful brands that focus on the rebels' market niche: in soft drinks, Jonas Soda; in shoes, Commander; etc.

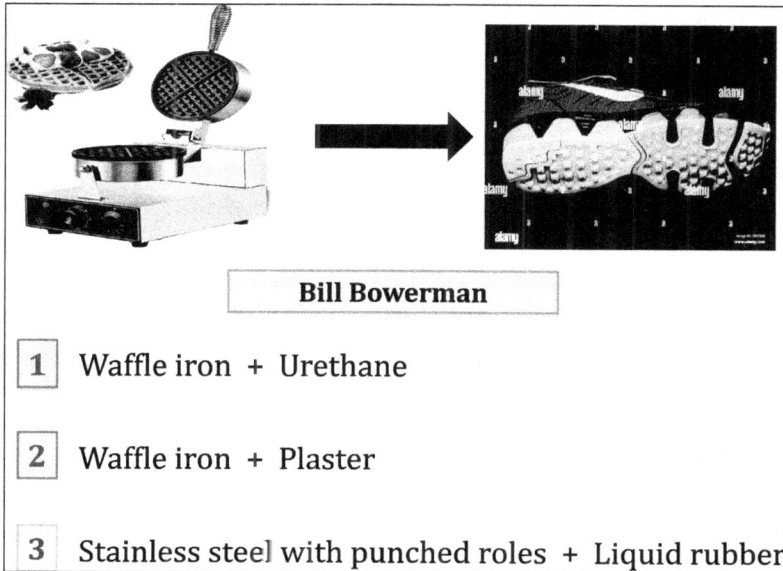

Bill Bowerman	
1	Waffle iron + Urethane
2	Waffle iron + Plaster
3	Stainless steel with punched roles + Liquid rubber

Figure 3 Bill Bowerman's path to the waffle-type sole innovation

So the shoes should stand out in terms of design. And the first Nike[11] shoes were creamy with blue stripes down the sides. In Phil Knight's words: "God, they were beautiful."[12]

---

[11]Originally, the company was named Blue Ribbon Sports. Only seven years after its foundation, in 1971, the name changed to Nike.
[12]This and other quotations to follow come from Shoe Dog by Phil Knight (2016).

A striking design was thus paramount. Not white, discreet, as most sneakers of the Converse brand or the Puma model used by Abebe Bikila, the winner of the Tokyo Olympic marathon in 1964.[13]

Outstanding was the common characteristic of all Nike's following models, for example, the 1966 Marup and the 1967/68 Cortez.[14]

1966: Marup model   *1967/68: Cortez model*

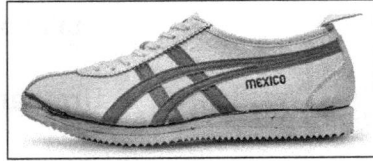

Besides *outstanding, lighter, comfortable,* and with a *strong grip,* with time came a fifth characteristic: **minimizing injuries**. Small rubber columns were inserted with a structure to cushion, to absorb the impact, inspired in shoeless runners—in the top part of the air pockets in the sole.

---

[13]The exceptions were some of Adidas models (such as the Olympiade) and Reebok.

[14]Today, naturally, we know more about the *personal characteristics of the average joggers.*

Besides **individualistic**, liking to be by themselves, loners, the opposite of team players, they tend to be **more educated** (doctors, engineers, etc.) and **wealthier** than the average population (participants in marathons have more years of education and earn more than average Americans).

Related to that is the fact that there is an **inverse relationship** between activity on the job and off it. The middle class that pushes pencils all day are more physical off the job.

However, for men and women who work hard in a factory all day doing heavy manual labor, it is harder to come home and decide that what they need is—to run for an hour.

Also joggers are more **urban**, as they need more the contact with nature that can be found in the parks of cities.

In sixth place, joggers are **highly professional**, compulsively dedicated to their work.

And finally (seventh), **more health-conscious** and consequently have longer life expectancy. They want both more life in the years and more years in the life.

Consequently, they are thinner (1 mile/1.6 km burns ± 120 calories), more likely to stop smoking and enjoy better health in general.

The final pillar of Nike's business theory (bottom line in Table 2) was the belief that importing from Japan would enable to **undercut Adidas** (the dominant company) **and other major brands' prices**. "Gentlemen," said Phil Knight at its first meeting at Japanese factory Onitsuka, "the American shoe market is enormous and largely untapped; if we price our shoes to undercut Adidas, which most American athletes now wear, it could be a hugely profitable venture."[15]

Here again Phil Knight noticed a start-up trend, importing the idea from the deep cuts made by the Japanese into the camera market that had once been dominated by Germans. *Why wouldn't Japanese running shoes do the same thing?*

The answer was no reason at all, and so in the late 1960s and 1970s, Japanese companies came to dominate many industries by entering via the **low-end** market segments—Canon in photocopying; Toyota, Mazda, and so on in cars; Suzuki and Kawasaki in motorcycles; Nissin Foods in prepared soups; Citizen in watches; and so on (Figure 4).

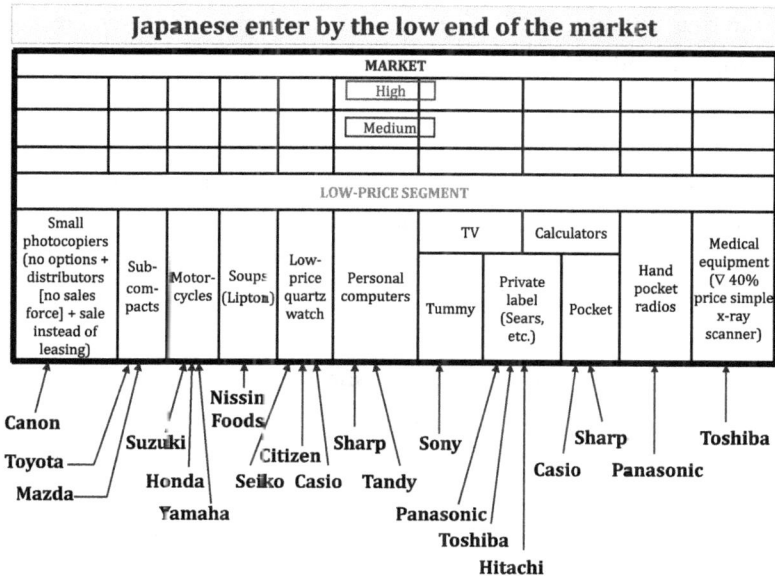

Japanese enter by the low end of the market

MARKET

High

Medium

LOW-PRICE SEGMENT

| Small photocopiers (no options + distributors [no sales force] + sale instead of leasing) | Sub-com-pacts | Motor-cycles | Soups (Lipton) | Low-price quartz watch | Personal computers | TV / Tummy | Calculators / Private label (Sears, etc.) | Pocket | Hand pocket radios | Medical equipment (∇ 40% price simple x-ray scanner) |

Canon
Toyota
Mazda
Suzuki — Honda — Yamaha
Nissin Foods
Citizen — Seiko — Casio
Sharp — Tandy
Sony — Panasonic — Toshiba — Hitachi
Sharp — Casio — Panasonic
Toshiba

Figure 4 Japanese enter by the low end of the market

---

[15]The first Nike's ad was a handout distributed all over Portland, which stressed that low Japanese labor costs made possible to offer shoes at the low price of $6.95!

Although much of the above may seem obvious **now**, à posteriori, when Phil Knight presented his idea to an entrepreneurship course at Stanford University, it was received with absolute **indifference** if not boredom. After having spent weeks preparing for his presentation, not one colleague, not a single soul, asked a question. In his words: "they greeted my passion and intensity with labored sighs and vacant stares."[16]

Another example that great ideas go through three stages: ridiculous, perhaps, and… finally…obvious.

And consequently, with time, all other brands started imitating Nike and making specialized shoes for runners (the total number of models featured in *Runner's World* magazine special edition increased from 16 in 1967 to 178 in 1979) while Nike on its own began making also differentiated sneakers for every sport, including for basketball: The first model was called Blazer and used by George Gervin, followed by other models such as Air Jordan for Michael Jordan.

It can thus be said that Nike was the first to recognize the several reality assumptions indicated before in Table 2.

To summarize, first of all, jogging was about to **boom**. Today, 15 percent of Americans (50 million) practice it. About 2 million run half marathons every year. Ten percent of Europeans (50 million) participate in running events (and the world's most sold type of watch is the smartwatch for fitness tracking: market value of 40 billion dollars).

Then, racing **required specialized sneakers,** and **there were no** good-enough specialized shoes. Next, specialized shoes should have **five characteristics** (lightness, comfort, gripping power, outstanding design, and minimizing injuries). And **Japan** could do in shoes what it was already doing in cameras and about to do in many other industries (from computers, to TVs, to calculators, to medical equipment, etc.)—see Table 2.

---

[16]To be fair to teachers, the Stanford professor gave an A in the course to Phil Knight.

The overall result of a **business theory** with reality assumptions that were not only (1) *true* and (2) *relevant* but also (3) *new* was that Nike overtook the two giants Adidas and Puma to such an extent that today its worth is more than **5 times** the former and **22 times** the latter.

2.2.2. The Other Variables of Nike's Business Plan Complementing the Theory of Business

Figure 1 (in Page 3 of the Introduction) indicated that a sound theory of business (the *why*) is a necessary, but not a sufficient condition for performance. Other three competitiveness drivers are necessary: sound strategies (*where*), business model (*what*), and tactics (*how*).

And so before moving on it is useful to look at how those three complemented Nike's theory of business.

Strategy involved the choice of (1) *geographical areas*, (2) *industries*, and (3) *segments*—the **where**.

In the specific case of Nike, the theory of business predetermined both the industry (sports shoes) and the segment (racing).[17] But the third element of strategy, the geography, was open to *decision*.

And Nike's choice was:

- First the city of *Portland*, that Phil Knight initially targeted with handouts and ads;
- Then the whole state of *Oregon*, with the presence at sports events; and
- The *Pacific Northwest*;
- Next came *California* chosen for proximity, climate, youth population, and purchasing power and served through a commissioned salesman in Seal Beach, Orange County;

---

[17]That is not always the case as the example of Better Place will later illustrate.

Portland ➡ Oregon state ➡ Pacific Northwest ➡ California ➡ USA ➡ Europe

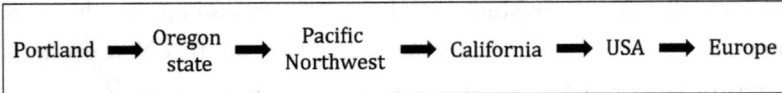

Figure 5 Nike's initial strategy in terms of geography

- To be followed by the *whole United States*, with marketing through industry fairs; and
- Finally, Nike went international starting with *Europe* (Figure 5).

With time Nike had to decide whether to **maintain** its strategy regarding *industry* (footwear), *segment* (sports shoes), and niche (running).

At first Nike stayed **focused**: one industry, one segment, one niche. Later, it **expanded** (to other segments and niches of the same industry), and finally **diversified** (into other, related, industries).[18]

Focus was done through several *models* (each one an improved version to serve the same need): the Cortez (for the 1968 Olympics) and the "waffle iron" model named Moon Shoe (in 1972), and so on.

Then in 1973 Nike **expanded** into new *niches* within the sports shoes segment. As mentioned, it expanded first into basketball with the Blazer model (used by NBA player George Gervin), followed by other models for the same segment such as Air Jordan (sponsored by Michael Jordan) and then further expanded into other niches such as skateboarding.

Still further **expansion** came with entry into other *segments* of the footwear industry: not sports shoes but casual sneakers for everyday use.

Under the influence of Farrah Fawcett of the TV show Charlie's Angels, Nike started offering several models for daily wear whose distinctive characteristics were (1) the image of a casual lifestyle, (2) sporty aesthetics, and (3) long-lasting comfort.

---

[18]Being a niche, a subset of a segment, that on its own a part of an industry, within a geographical area.

And then *within this new casual segment* Nike served the *five niches* of classic everyday sneakers (with, for example, Nike Air Force 1, Nike Blazer mid-77), lightweight and sporty (Nike Free RN and Nike Waffle One), comfort focused (Nike Pegasus and Nike Renew Ride 3), low price (Nike Tanjun and Nike Downshifter 12), and stylish pics (Nike SB Dunk Low and Nike Air Max 90).

Finally, Nike **diversified** into *industries* related to footwear—first into *sportswear* starting with jackets: a lightweight model called Windrunner that quickly became a favorite both on the street and on the track due to its stylish design.

This was followed by the *apparel equipment industry*: speed ropes, hairbands, backpacks, duffel bags, water bottles, and so on.[19]

Once having defined both **theory of business** and **strategy**, the next step is to specify the **business model:** the *basic pillars of operations* to *transform* client satisfaction (derived from the theory of business) in certain areas (due to strategy), into *company value*.

A **business model** is basically the foundations, the organization stepping stones a company uses to make a profit. Its profit formula. The processes needed to deliver the offering.[20]

In Nike's early years, those *processes* were **four** (Figure 6):

1. *All manufacturing* (including packaging) *outsourced*;
2. To a *single entity*: Onitsuka factory in Japan;

---

[19]The strategy and the theory of business must always be compatible. As companies move along with time and environmental changes, if one changes, one must assess what is the impact on the other. Is there a fit?

[20]As stressed before, it can be argued that a *business model* respects to *how* a company operates. That is correct. However, since a business model focuses on the fundamental pillars, the stepping stones, it is also a synthesis, a summary of operations. Thus, it is better to define the **business model** as the **what** to distinguish it from the **how**, which are the detailed **tactics** of the several functional areas: human resources, marketing, finance, accounting, information systems, and so on: how to recruit, train, advertise, finance, set up the cost accounting system, and so on.

3. *Direct to Consumer (DTC) marketing*; with
4. The *same channels* playing the *multiple* roles of promotion, selling (getting orders), and delivery.

It is frequent for new ventures to outsource manufacturing.

It is less common for that outsourcing:

- To involve *everything*, even packaging, that is: to be total;
- To be done to a *single* entity; and
- Both during an extended period (for 10 years, from 1964 to 1974, until Nike established a factory in New Hampshire, United States, marking Nike's direct involvement in manufacturing).

The **second pillar** of the business model was that all the above was done with the *single entity* of Onitsuka factory in Japan. Only.

Japan was chosen because of the theory of business (low labor costs and quality of manufacturing), and *Onitsuka* was singled out for two other reasons:

- It had a reputation for quality (it was already selling wrestling shoes in the northeastern United States); and
- On top of wrestling, basketball, and discus shoes (for athletes competing in discus-throwing events), Onitsuka was already manufacturing tracking sneakers.

Over time, both Onitsuka and Japan would be replaced, due to rising labor costs and other reasons,[21] sequentially by South Korea, Taiwan, China, Indonesia, and Vietnam, and Nike abandoned its single supplier policy.

Marketing was all DTC, with no intermediaries, for the simple reason that no sports stores, much less large chains, wanted to carry the Nike brand.

---

[21]There was a mutual lawsuit that lasted for 1 year between Onitsuka and Nike.

Adidas dominated the market. And Puma, Reebok, and Converse were also prestigious players. So, "Kid, what this world does not need is another track shoes," was the standard rejection to P. Knight by sporting goods stores.

DTC marketing was such a strong pillar of Nike's initial business model that it became part of its **DNA**. Even today, the company relies heavily on DTC channels, including its *own retail stores* and *digital platforms*, since they allow for greater control over customer experience and provide useful consumer data.

Also within DTC marketing, channels can play simultaneously the multiple roles of promotion, selling (getting orders), and sometimes even delivery.[22]

With the exception of the very early stages when promotion was done by handouts and ads in Portland and delivery was consequently separated, Phil Knight opted for **channels playing multiple roles** (track meetings, industry fairs, and commissioned salesmen) and thus saving the scarce resources of money, time, and manpower (Figure 6).

In short, not all marketing is direct, and in any case DTC can be done through channels playing either multiple or specialized roles (as can non-direct marketing).

---

[22]As in other times, that is not the case, and it may be useful to go into **some details**, here.

When a company opts for DTC using no intermediaries, no third parties, either for promotion (e.g., advertising agencies, public relations companies) or for selling (independent stores) or for delivery by third parties, DTC channels can nevertheless be specialized *or* play multiple functions.

If a company does internally its ads and handouts to reach the final clients, then promotion is DTC but not necessarily the selling (getting orders) or delivery.

In the case of Nike, going to track meetings (Phil Knight at first and then through exclusive commissioned salesmen) played three roles all together: promotion, selling, and delivery (on the spot, from own trucks).

And industry fairs played the dual role of promotion and selling (obtaining orders), but not of delivery.

Nike, however, opted both for *direct marketing* and, within this, for channels playing *multiple roles* (Figure 6).

Thus, there were **four building blocks to Nike's business model**: (1) *total outsourcing*, (2) to a *single entity*, (3) *DTC marketing*, and (4) with same channels playing *multiple roles*.

6.1. Nike's business model

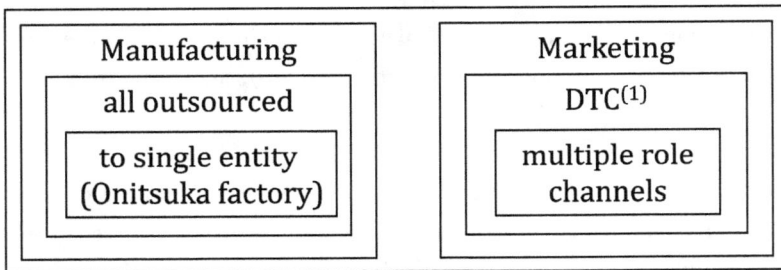

Manufacturing	Marketing
all outsourced	DTC[1]
to single entity (Onitsuka factory)	multiple role channels

6.2. Detail of Nike's direct marketing

Nike's direct marketing Channels	Roles played by own channels	Promotion	Selling (getting orders)	Delivery (on the spot)
Ads and handouts distributed in Portland		Yes	No	No
Track meets through	Philip Knight	Yes	Yes	Yes
	Own commissioned salesmen			
Industry fairs		Yes	Yes	No

(1) Direct to Consumer.

Figure 6 Nike's business model and detail of direct marketing

While as per Figure 1 in Page 3 both the *business model* and *strategy* implement the *theory of business*, they both on their own impact on **tactics,** which is the fourth competitiveness driver. And so Nike's tactics are listed on the right-side column of Figure 7.

Theory of Business (reality assumptions)		Business Model	Tactics
1. Running is about to **boom**	On track—Competition	1. **All** Manufacturing outsourced, including packaging	1. **Low price:** $6.95
	Off track—Joggers		2. **Ads** and **handouts** pitch/text
2. Racing requires **specialized** shoes		2. To **Onitsuka** factory in Japan	3. **Product:** creamy with blue stripes
3. Specialized shoes should have **five** characteristics	Light	3. **DTC** (direct-to-consumer marketing)	4. **Packaging** standing out: orange colour
	Comfortable		
	Minimizing injuries	4. **Multiple roles** channels marketing	5. **Track** meetings
	Gripping power		6. Own **commissioned** salesmen
	Outstanding design		
4. There **were no** good-enough specialized shoes			7. Industry **fairs**
5. It was possible **to undercut** market players prices through Japanese imports			8. **Large-supply orders** (to obtain scale economies)
			9. **Nissho** Trading Co

Figure 7 Nike at upstart

Tactics is the realm of the **how** and refers to the *functional areas*, which are nine in total: (1) marketing, (2) finance, (3) human resources, (4) operations/production, (5) accounting, (6) information systems, (7) administration (maintenance, hygiene security, etc.), (8) general management (organization chart, control and coordination devices, rules and procedures), and (9) R&D.

And regardless of the specific functional area, there are **two** types of tactics as per Figure 8.

First are those that directly **implement** the theory of business and the business model (in Figure 7, all except Tactics Numbers 8 and 9, namely, large supply orders and Nissho Trading Co.), and the second are those that **must** nevertheless be **executed,** as **otherwise** the business will enter into disruption.

The two types of tactics — Area / Type	Marketing	Operations	...	R&D
Directly **implement** the business theory and business model	**Excellence** required			
Other	**Satisfactorily** executed to avoid disruptions			

Figure 8 The two types of tactics

The former requires *excellence*. The latter must be done in a *satisfactory* way. Otherwise, the business is put at risk (the strength of a chain is the strength of its weakest link).

An example was Nike's policy of overextending the *size of its orders* to suppliers in disproportionate amounts to the existing clients' orders.

As a consequence, Nike was frequently cash-strapped and courting bankruptcy: "*we are not broke, we just don't have any money*"—Phil Knight used to reassure his partner B. Bowerman so frequently that at a certain point his wife started refusing to hear his complaints: "*here comes the wall.*"[23]

Another example that functional policies simply require is *satisfactory* execution (not *excellence*) when they do not derive from the business theory and business model was in the financial area.

---

[23]In Phil Knight's words, Nike was constantly in the risk of bankruptcy because: "*I was to blame. I refused to consider ordering less inventory. Why cut an order from 3 down to 2 million if I believed the demand out there is for 5 million? Thus I would order a number of shoes that seemed absurd and we'd need to stretch to pay for. To most observers this would've seemed a brazenly reckless, dangerous way of doing business, but I believed demand was greater than sales.*"

Here, Nike worked for long mostly with the First National Bank. But then at a certain point, relations soured with not only Nike for lack of cash, being a few days away from bankruptcy, but this even involved a complaint to the FBI. Were it not for the decisive intervention of the Japanese trading company *Nissho*, Nike would have gone under.

However, the **most important tactics** are those that being a direct consequence of those that *implement* the business theory and model (all examples indicated in Figure 7, except the bottom two with numbers 8 and 9) discussed before. Here, *excellence* is required.

The first model of shoes (Onitsuka Tiger) was very *low priced* at $6.95 to undercut competition (a direct consequence of the fifth reality assumption of the business theory).

And so, the pitch of the earliest *ads and handouts* enhanced that: *Best news in flats! Japan challenges European track domination... low Japanese labor costs make it possible to offer shoes at low, low, prices.*

Both the sneakers and the packaging stood out. The *shoes* were creamy with blue stripes. And the *packaging*, the boxes, were *"of bright neon orange ... the boldest color in the rainbow ... in those days shoe boxes were either white or blue, period, but I (Phil Knight), wanted something that would stand out... pop on the shelves."*

DTC and multiple roles channels meant, besides *own commissioned salespeople,*[24] two types of events: *track meetings* and *industry fairs*.

Both were highly successful. At track meets after *"showing my wares I couldn't write orders fast enough."*

And at industry fairs (e.g., Chicago), *"the mob of salesmen would pick up the Nikes, held them to the light, touched the swoosh and ... liked it a whole*

---

[24]The first of which was for a long time Jeff Johnson in Seal Beach, California.

lot, they gave us business, actually placed orders with us, exceeding our grand-est expectations."

In short, together with *strategy* it was:

- The **soundness** of Nike's *theory of business, business model,* and *tactics*;
- Their **novelty** (which allowed for differentiation); and
- How they all were **linked**, fit, together (one logically following from the **other**) that explain Nike's success: Within 16 years, Nike attained 50 percent market share in the U.S. athletic shoe market and then went public later that year.

And all that started in the mid-1960s. But, astonishing as that success was, it was… a long time ago.

And so the question arises of the **relevance in today's world of the four competitiveness drivers** (and of the models presented in Figure 1 of Page 3 and in further detail in Table 1 of Page 9).

After all, the world has changed considerably, specially recently due to the digital revolution.

As *Philip Kotler*, known as the father of modern marketing, refers in his memoirs, *the digital revolution created new paradigms and destroyed others.*

Thus, the **question: Do the above models still hold in the age of the net?** And do they apply to net-based companies?

The answer is **yes**, exemplified by *Dollar Shave Club* in Section 2.3.

Founded by Michael Dubin, it achieved *unicorn status* in just five years in an industry (grooming) dominated by two giants: Gillette and Schick, at a certain point with **70 percent** of market share.

2.3. Dollar Shave Club Against Gillette (and Schick)

2.3.1. The Theory of Business

As said, the grooming market had for long been dominated by Gillette and Schick. They were the 500-pound gorillas and so they charged in the vicinity of 20 dollars for 4 or 5 blades.[25]

As high-priced small items tend to disappear from supermarket shelves… the solution was to place them behind the checkout counter or in closed drawers.

That created (on top of the **high price**) the inconvenience, the **hassle**, of having to ask the cashier for the blades or ask an employee to open the drawer.

And so it went for a long time until Michael Dubin saw **five things** in reality.

From the (1) *high prices* and (2) *inconvenience* the customers were subject to, followed (3) a feeling of injustice, of **unfairness**, of almost…being ripped-off.[26]

Then (4) blades are a commodity item with a manufacturing **cost** far below the selling price (indeed the first blades that Michel Dubin sold were imported at very low prices from South Korea).

And finally there was no need for the inconvenience of in-store shopping, since **home delivery** was becoming ever more popular for all sorts

---

[25]The razor being quite inexpensive, just as printers prices are low, comparative to those of cartridges.

[26]The field of behavioral economics/prospect theory which in recent decades produced two Nobel Prize winners (D. Kahneman and R. Thaler) emphasizes fairness as one of the heuristics: behavioral traits people use spontaneously.

Thus, the negative consumer reaction to Uber attempt in some U.S. cities to raise prices during snow storms. Also to the First Chicago Bank charging customers a fee for dealing with a bank teller instead of using an ATM.

And Dougles Ivester, CEO of Coca-Cola, was fired when he flirted with the idea of vending machines prices to vary with temperature.

of products: from groceries to food, to pharmacy items. Glovo delivers almost everything. Bolt also. And Uber extensively so.

Consequently, Dollar Shave Club created a home delivery service initially only for razors and blades and afterward including other grooming products such as foams, aftershaves, skin creams, deodorants, and so on, with the client being able to select among several subscription plans starting with two blades/razors for $1 per month.[27]

Table 3 summarizes Michael Dubin's Dollar Shave Club *five reality assumptions (the business theory)*:

1. Market prices for blades were far **too inflated**;
2. The shopping experience was **cumbersome**;
3. Both the above factors **upset** the clients creating (an underestimated and untapped) feeling of unfairness;
4. Blades are **commodities**; and
5. **Home delivery** was easily implementable.

The theory of business was the upstart for Dollar Shave Club to achieve **unicorn**[28] status in **five** years only and **51 percent** of online market share; in view of its success, both Gillette and Schick rapidly went online too, followed by other smaller competitors.

But then followed the *business model, strategy, and tactics*.

Table 3 Dollar Shave Club theory of business (reality assumptions) at upstart (2011)

1	Blades **prices** are inflated
2	In-store blades buying is a **hassle**
3	People **resent** both of the above
4	Blades are **commodities**
5	**Home delivery** of blades is feasible

---

[27]Annual contracts.
[28]A company worth at least $1 billion.

2.3.2. Dollar Shave Club Business Model, Strategy, and Tactics Complementing the Business Theory

The **business model** was characterized by:

1. *Large imports* from *South Korea* to undercut market prices;
2. Service flexibility through several monthly *subscription plans*;
3. Promotion using the *net* (to keep costs *low*); and
4. Customer *low risk*: money-back guarantee and the possibility of canceling at any time[29] (besides very low price).

Then there was **strategy**. *Geographically*, it meant first the United States, followed by Canada and Australia, and, in 2016, Unilever acquired Dollar Shave Club further extending its global reach.

In terms of *segments and industries*, strategy meant initially focus on a single segment (blades/razors) of the grooming industry and then sequential *expansion* into other segments and *diversification* into other industries:

- Shaving accessories (creams, gels, foams and aftershaves);
- Body care products (body washers, lotions and moisturizers);
- Hair care (shampoos, conditioners and styling products);
- Oral care (now <u>beyond</u> the grooming industry and into toothbrushes toothpaste and mouth wash);
- Skin care (face cleansers, moisturizers and serums); and finally
- Fragrances (both colognes and body sprays).

Also segments evolved not only in terms of products but in terms of *clients* as well: After young males, young females were targeted too.

Finally, there were the **tactics**. *Selling* through several subscription plans (for various amounts of blades/razors),[30] which at a later stage included

---

[29]At the start; later a fidelization program was introduced.
[30]With the policies of money-back guaranteed and the possibility of canceling at any time to minimize customer risk.

options for other grooming products and the introduction of a fidelization program.

The initial *pricing* of penetration, not skimming, with the cheapest option of
two blades per month for $1, was making no money (delivery was free), but
it had two advantages: It enabled scale to decrease costs and opened the door
to higher-priced subscription alternatives (topped by the "executive plan").

Logistics involved a large warehouse, specialized machinery, and a considerable number of manpower reaching soon 600 employees.

Net promotion (one of the business model pillars) was done by a website
linked to bloggers and a series of low-budget ($4,500) extremely funny
videos that became viral: The first film sold 250,000 blades in 72 hours,
the site collapsed in the first night, and it had 27 million viewers.

And *product policy* (one of the 4Ps of the marketing mix) was also original.
Contrary to Gillette that launched razors for women different from those
to men (the *sensor brand*), Dollar Shave Club targeted both men and
women <u>exactly</u> with the same type of blades and razors and stressed that
equality in the net.

Thus, the *Dollar Shave Club's success* of 4 million subscribers, unicorn status within five years, and 51 percent of market share[31] can be attributed
to the quality of the **four** competitiveness drivers: the *theory of business*,
the *business model*, *strategy*, and *tactics*. To **all four**. Indicating that not
only **all** remain **relevant** in the digital age but also that **they apply to
net-based companies**. It seems thus that **the Four Drivers Model remains today as actual as ever** (Figure 9).

However, both sneakers and blades can be seen as *relatively simple products*. That raises the question whether a sound theory of business is also a

---

[31]After Dollar Shave Club reached 3 million subscribers, Gillette and other market players started offering home delivery, too. That did not prevent, however, the
company from having 51 percent of *online* market share.

Theory of Business (reality assumptions)	Business model	Tactics
1. Blades prices are inflated	1. Large imports from South Korea enable to undercut prices	1. Money back-guarantee
2. In-store buying is a hassle	2. Service flexibility through several subscription plans	2. Possibility of cancelling any time
3. Customers resent both the above	3. Low-cost net promotion	3. Free delivery
4. Blades are commodities	4. Low customer risk	4. Several subscription plans
5. Home delivery is feasible		5. Low-cost price plan at one dollar for market penetration
		6. Large warehouse with specialized machinery and extensive manpower
		7. Website linked to blogs
		8. Series of low-cost funny ads
		9. Product equal for male and female
		10. Ads stressing that equality

Figure 9 Dollar Shave Club at upstart

prerequisite for success in *intensive know-how businesses*. Such as the **space industry**, for instance.

2.4. How SpaceX Came to Dominate the Space Industry[32]

Few industries deal with products as expensive and technologically complex as the aerospace.

Thus, its players are either state-owned companies or large multinationals, theoretically private, but frequently dependent on taxpayers money through subsidies. Examples are Lockheed and Boeing, which later joined forces to create United Launch Alliance (ULA), Arianespace in Europe, Long March in China, and several Russian companies (Beriev, Ilyushin, Yakolev, or Tupolev).

So, how can a start-up with limited own, private, funds make a dent in such an industry and against the deep pockets of competitors?

The answer is by detecting in reality **facts that others fail to see**. Thus, developing a different theory of business. And creating a company grounded on that.

The first fact *SpaceX* was built upon was that **3 billion people**, the world's poorest, did not have access to Internet. They simply could not afford it.

Why? As optic cables were not an option for poor countries such as Chad or the Republic of Congo, or still for isolated ones such as Papua New Guinea and American Samoa, that left the alternative of satellites, which if powerful and expensive required the acquisition of large antennas to receive the signals.

Or, when they are cheaper and feebler, they allowed for solar-powered lower-price and smaller antennas to receive the signals.

---

[32]In order to simplify, in the SpaceX example, one will exclusively focus on the business theory.

And that was the focus of SpaceX, which aimed at being **the low cost of space**. In E. Musk's words: *"the southwest airlines of space."*[33]

The **second** and **third** reality assumptions followed from the first: *clients* and *technology*.

On clients the belief that **poor** and **isolated countries** were eager on buying Internet for communications, weather forecast, and even research (transporting scientists for lab stations in orbit).

And that there were a second type of clients, namely some **companies** in rich countries (Canadians, Europeans, Asian) that could not afford the high prices prevailing in the market; nevertheless, they wanted to benefit from satellites services for Internet, TV, radio, weather, research, navigation, or imaging.[34]

The third assumption was *technological*—that well-functioning satellites could be far cheaper than what the industry was providing. Market players were providing Ferraris, while a Honda Accord would do the job: *Rockets had to be low cost and satellites smaller in size.*

And that required a **business model** characterized by (1) *high vertical integration for cost control*, (2) adaptation of *already existing electronics products* (instead of creating them anew), (3) *lean manufacturing processes* including the use of the same components in different versions of rockets, and (4) *reusable rockets.*

In further detail:

First: great **vertical integration**. By opposition to competitors that relied upon a large number of suppliers (1,200 in the case of ULA, the joint

---

[33]From Elon Musk's biography by Ashlee Vance (2015) and also the same titled biography by Walter Isaacson (2023).

[34]Satellites can zoom, for example, on Iowa and determine which corn fields are ready for harvest, or in the parking lot of large supermarkets to calculate the number of cars.

venture between Lockheed and Boeing), SpaceX builds in-house 80 to 90 percent of its rockets and spacecraft, thus achieving through vertical integration greater control over the manufacturing process and cost management.

Second: SpaceX uses already **available** consumer electronics and adapts them as need be, instead of space-grade equipment as others in the industry. The same logic applies to, for example, tanks for fuel from tanks manufacturers not previously associated with the space industry.

Third: small (not truck-sized) **satellites.** As of 2023 SpaceX has 5,000 small satellites in low-height orbit (from 40 km to 1,200 km) providing Internet services.

Fourth: low-price rockets initially in-house built, modular approach (using common components across different versions of rockets), and efficient manufacturing processes and later through reusable rocket technology.

That allows rockets to be used in multiple flights, just as planes are not discarded away after trips but are always in use 24/7.

These are the **four** main characteristics of SpaceX *business model* which implemented the business theory of being the low-cost producer, the Southwest Airlines of the space industry (Figure 10).

From the above, results followed: valued at $210 billion, SpaceX is today worth more than any other aerospace and defense company.[35]

And although the first profit was turned only in the first quarter of 2023 (55 million, more than two decades after its foundation in 2002), in 2023 SpaceX made nearly 100 launches (far above that of any competitor) and has 5,000 small and low-cost SpaceX satellites in orbit, making SpaceX

---

[35]SpaceX is traded not publicly, but only in the secondary market.

Theory of Business (reality assumptions)	Business Model
1. Three billion people (the world poorer) cannot access/afford internet	1. Vertical integration for cost control
2. Clients: Poorer countries; Isolated countries; Rich countries companies not willing to pay top prices	2. Adaptation of already existing electronics
3. Technologically feasible to provide satellite services with "Honda Accords besides Ferraris" → 3.1. Low-cost rockets; 3.2. Small (not truck-sized) satellites	3. Efficient manufacturing processes, including common components across different types of rockets
	4. Reusable rockets

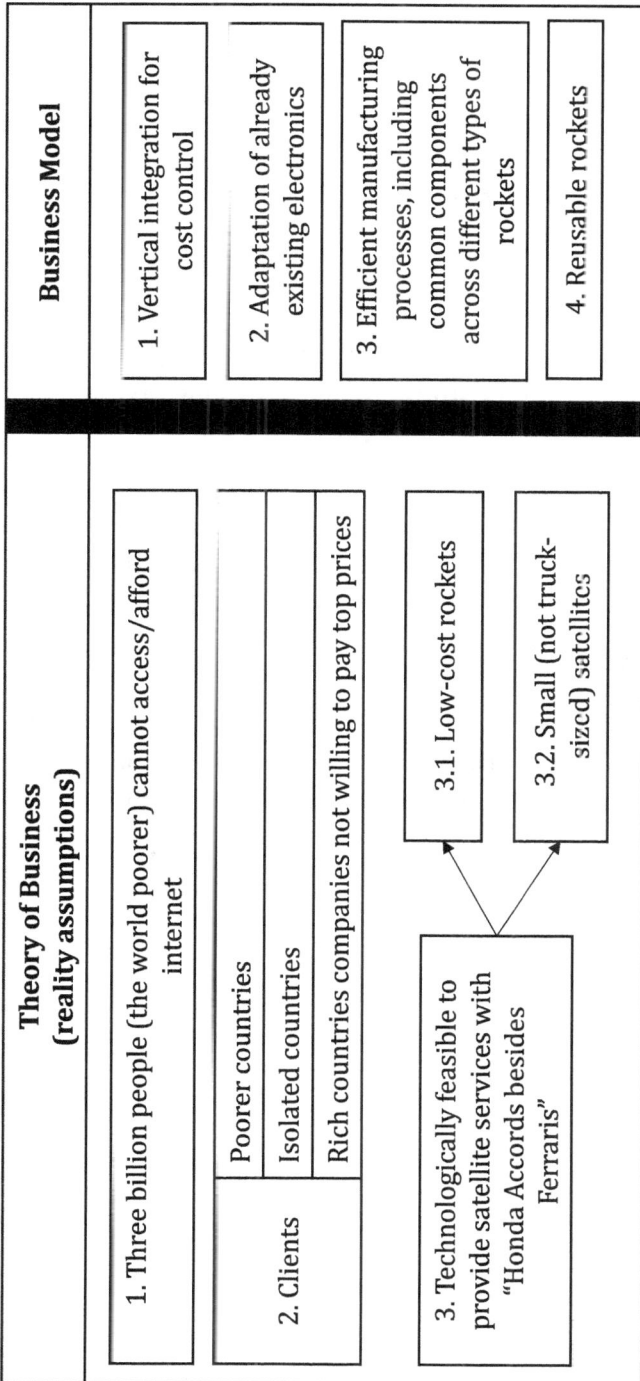

Figure 10 SpaceX theory of business

dominance best seen by its market share in quantitative terms (percentage of satellites):

- SpaceX: 50 percent
- Oneweb satellites: 7 percent
- Chinese government: 5 percent
- US government: 4 percent
- Etc.

2.5. Putting Together the Three Examples of Nike, Dollar Shave Club, and SpaceX

This chapter focused on three **distinct examples**.

Dollar Shave Club is a low-price commodity supplier. *Nike* provides products with a price range from several dozens to hundreds of dollars. And that of SpaceX is in the hundreds of millions. And naturally that technical complexity increases with price.

Nevertheless, all three examples share the **common traits** of a (1) *clear*, (2) *valid*, (3) *relevant*, and (4) *novel* theory of business (Figure 11). The **first three** characteristics are a **must**, fundamental for a company to survive. The **fourth** is a further **advantage,** as it facilitates differentiation from competition.

Nike's theory of business was grounded upon:

1. Racing (both off-track—joggers—and on-track—competition) was about to **boom**;
2. Racing required **specialized** shoes;
3. There were **no** good-enough specialized shoes;
4. Specialized shoes should have **five** characteristics:
    4.1. As light as possible;
    4.2. Comfortable;
    4.3. Minimizing injuries;
    4.4. With gripping power;
    4.5. An appealing design; and
5. It was possible with Japanese imports to **undercut** the prices of the dominant market players.

Nike	Dollar Shave Club	SpaceX
1. Running is booming — On track (competition) / Off track (joggers)	1. Blades prices are high — Inflated to cost / Causing resentment	1. Three billion people cannot afford Internet
2. Racing requires specialized shoes	2. In-store buying is a hassle	2. Unserved clients — Countries: Poor / Isolated; Some companies of rich countries
3. Specialized shoes should have five characteristics — Light / Comfortable / Minimizing injuries / Gripping power / Outstanding design	3. People resent the above	3. It is both technically and economically possible to be a low-cost satellite service provider
4. There were no good-enough specialized shoes	4. Blades are commodities	
5. Japanese shoes can undercut prices of dominant players	5. Home delivery of blades is feasible	

Figure 11 *Reality assumptions of the three examples*

Then **Dollar Shave Club** business theory was based on:

1. Blades prices are **inflated**;
2. In-store buying is a **hassle**;
3. People **resent** both the above;
4. Blades are **commodities**;
5. **Home delivery** of blades is feasible.

Finally, **SpaceX** started with the following assumptions:

1. **Three** billion people cannot afford Internet;
2. **Unserved** clients are (A) the poorer countries, (B) isolated countries, and (C) some companies in rich countries; and
3. It is technologically and economically possible to create "the **Southwest Airlines** of the space industry."

Thus, the number of reality assumptions of a business theory varies. Five in the case of Nike. The same in Dollar Shave Club. And three in SpaceX.

And as a last point, it is interesting to note that those reality **beliefs** have **different** natures (Figure 12).

Three are **statistical** in nature:

- Nike's that running was booming;
- Dollar Shave Club's on the high prices of blades; and
- SpaceX's that 3 billion people could not afford net.

Other **three** are **judgmental**:

- Nike: There were no good-enough specialized sneakers for jogging and that Japanese shoes could undercut prices of dominant players; and of
- SpaceX regarding the type of unserved clients.

Type of assumptions \ Company	Nike	Dollar Shave Club	SpaceX
Statistical	Running is booming	High blades prices	Three billion unserved customers
Market judgments	No good specialized sneakers		Type of customers willing to buy low price net
	Japanese shoes can undercut prices of market players		
Client's psychology		In-store buying is a bother	
		People resent both the high prices and the inconvenience	
Technical	Racing requires specialized shoes	Blades are commodities	It is possible to create a low-price segment
	Specialized shoes should have five characteristics	Home delivery is feasible	

Figure 12 The different nature of the reality assumptions of the business theory

Two are about the **psychology** of the client:

- Dollar Shave Club's assumption that in-store buying is a bother and that customers resent both the high prices and the inconvenience of in-store buying.

Finally, **five assumptions** are **technical** in their nature:

- For Nike: Racing requires specialized shoes and they should have the five characteristics of light, comfortable, minimizing injuries, gripping power, and outstanding design;
- For Dollar Shave Club: Blades are a commodity, and home delivery of blades is possible; and
- For SpaceX: It was possible to create a low market end in the space industry (to be the "Southwest Airlines of space").

Later on, Chapter 4 will discuss that regardless of their nature, all assumptions must be periodically tested to confirm the actuality of the theory of business on which the organization is grounded.

But, of course, the **type** of tests and how **easy** it is to make them vary according to the nature of the reality hypothesis.

Statistical are the easiest. Next are market judgments. *Client's psychology and technical assumptions* are hardest but still possible with behavioral interviews, direct emotional assessments, key success factors analysis, and comparative analysis with other industries, all techniques to be analyzed in Chapter 4.

2.6. Conclusion: From the Business Theory to the Business Model

Although a **solid** *theory of business* that is (1) *clear,* (2) *true,* (3) *relevant,* and preferably (4) *novel* is necessary, it is not a sufficient condition for performance. It is not enough by itself.

A **sound** *business model* is also necessary.

The theory of business indicates how to create *value for the client.* The business model defines how to create *value for the company.*

So, unless the business model *fits* the theory of business, customer value will not be translated into company profits.

To illustrate that indeed it is so is the next chapter's task with the help of the cases of McDonald's, SolarCity, and Spotify.

CHAPTER 3

Business Model: Why It Took Nearly Two Decades for Spotify to Achieve Profitability (While SolarCity Revolutionized Its Industry from the Start)

The best big idea is only going to be as good as its implementation.

(Jay Samit)

3.1. Introduction

While the **theory of business** is the organization's *beliefs about reality*, a **business model** is the basic organization *pillars to get an important job done*: creating value for the company while serving the client.

The **first time** the term "business model" was used was in the academic article "On the Construction of a Multi-Stage, Multi-Person Business Game" by R. Bellman and others in 1957.[36]

The term came into disuse until the 2000s when it was resuscitated by M. Porter, M. Simpson, C. Christensen, and others.[37]

It is telling, however, that the pioneers, Bellman and others, who introduced the term, did it in a review called Operations Research.

And so at the heart, at the very core of the concept of a business model, are **operations**, the organization to perform key activities.[38] Not the problem, neither the need.

Although with time other terms came to be associated with business model,[39] such as the value chain and canvas (an instrument to operationalize and visualize it),[40] at the center of a business model is how a company plans to make a profit, to create value: the **business profit formula**. How, while providing value for the client, the company creates value for itself.

---

[36]Bellman et al. (1957).

[37]The term "business model" has been wrongly associated with P. Drucker's HBR (Sept.–Oct.) 1994 article, but Drucker never uses it. He only speaks of theory of business. Never business model.

[38]Details regard tactics (marketing, finance, and so on, all functional areas) as addressed previously and Chapter 6 will do so in more detail.

[39]Several works recognize that the business model is "frequently confused with other popular terms" (e.g., Peric et al., 2017), while others point out the "lack of consensus on a definition of business model" (e.g., Bigelow and Barney, 2021).

[40]Alexander Osterwalder with Yves Pigneur introduced Canvas in his book *Business Model Generation* (2010). Canvas provides a visual tool to describe, analyze, and design business models, which has been extensively used in literature, for example, in the information and communications technology (Koprivnjak et al., 2020).

Thus, the **relationship** between a business model and the theory of business has **three** main characteristics.

First, they are *different concepts*. While the theory of business is not within, at the interior, but *outside* a firm, in its relation with reality, being the bridge between both, the business model respects the *inside* of an organization.

Second, both *are necessary but neither of them are sufficient* conditions for performance, competitiveness.

The previous chapter exemplified the importance of a theory of business adhering to reality. Unless it is cement solidly gluing the company to reality, there is no reason for its existence.

But then it is through the business model that the organization delivers, gets the job done.

And that (**third**) regardless if the theory of business is *new* (an innovation) or *not* (the organization faces competition).

An example of the *former* is the chain of **Minute Clinic** with its advertising: *Nobody is patient when having a fever*. And therefore the slogan: *You are sick, we are quick.*

Here, the business model has to be built around speed, what requires the possibility of visiting a doctor's office without an appointment and making nurses 24/7 available to treat minor health issues.

An example of the *latter* is the **iPod** and the **iTunes**. At a certain point they accounted for almost 50 percent of Apple's revenue catapulting Apple's market capitalization from $7 billion (in 2003) to $150 billion (in late 2007).

However, the first companies to bring digital music players to the market were Diamond Multimedia and Best Data.

Apple's real innovation was to make downloading digital music extremely easy through a novel combination of hardware and software.

In short, the theory of business and the business model are *distinct*, they *complement* each other, and both are *indispensable* for performance. And the present chapter will provide examples that it is so.[41]

First, **Spotify** will illustrate that even if a theory of business is sound, the business model has serious flaws—profits will fail to appear until needed corrections are introduced to, what happened after two decades (*next section*).

To correct the business model is thus a must. Sometimes it requires the change of a single key activity, and **McDonald's** will illustrate that (*Section 3.3*).

Other times more than one key variable must be altered, and **SolarCity** is a case in point (*in Section 3.4*).

Whatever, the above examples leave open the question of **how** to optimize the business model (and the theory of business), a task to be addressed in the following chapters.

For now, let's look at how a deficient business model can destroy a great theory of business.

3.2. Spotify: How a Faulty Business Model Prevented Performance (for Nearly Two Decades)

Spotify, created in 2006, launched its market platform in 2008.

And at the date we write (early 2025), its history can be divided into two parts.

---

[41]A review of business model literature can be summarized under two tenets:
- Generalized recognition of the business model importance (e.g., Gassmann et al., 2014; Koprivnjak et al.. 2020) even to the point that it is "rapidly replacing strategy as the most significant source of competitive advantage" (Snihur and Eisenhardt, 2022); and
- "confusion with other popular terms" (Peric et al., 2017) due to a "lack of consensus on a definition of business model" (Bigelow et al., 2021).

A first period until the beginning of 2022 (*"you should not expect that we are going to go back to 2021 behavior,"* said Daniel Ek, Spotify's founder and CEO, signaling the cut point), and a second period henceforth which culminated with net profits (positive bottom line) in 2024 (1.1 billion euros).

Given the CEO's statement on policies and their lag time effect, a cut point should be considered around 1/1/2022.

3.2.1. The First Period of Spotify: From 2006 to the Start of 2022

During this period, **Spotify dominated** the music streaming business with its revenue reaching near 10 billion euros against $7 billion of Apple Music (its most important competitor) and far above the $200 million of other players such as Tidal.

Among the over 500 million music streaming subscribers, Spotify's market share was 2.5 to 3 times that of any of the three most relevant competitors (Apple Music, Amazon Music, and YouTube Music) with other companies either discontinued (Google Music 2011–2020), far less relevant (Tidal, Napster), or still pirates (Pirate Bay, etc.).

Then on top of Spotify dominating the music streaming business, it had a **sound theory of business**: Its reality assumptions were (and remain) (1) true, (2) relevant, and (still better) (3) innovative.

First, many people *like* to listen to music. In the United States, 93 percent do so, spending into it more hours than watching TV (20.1 hours per week in 2022) and increasingly more so (in 2021 it was 18.4 hours).

Also, most people listen to music by *streaming*: 80 percent, what represents a new trend regarding the recent past of CDs and DVDs with two-thirds of the music industry revenue by streaming (both paid subscription and ad-supported).

And *finally*, not only many people like to listen to music and do so by streaming, but they were also *willing to* pay, instead of using pirate sites.

In 2021, the subscriber number of over 500 million had increased tenfold since 2015 with an annual revenue growth rate of around 35 percent, making up for a total streaming revenue of around $17 billion.

Sure enough that users of pirate music sites remained numerous: Even in 2021, there were around 15 billion visits. However and in spite of the increase in world population, the overall music piracy fell by more than half since 2017,[42] the reasons being ethical concerns and the qualities of legal sites: accessibility, convenience, affordable pricing, vast music library, the possibility of personalization with curated playlists, among others.

In short, Spotify has been the dominant market player. And its *theory of business* assumptions were *supported by empirical evidence*.

So, how come Spotify's net income (bottom line) was negative during 18 consecutive years (2006–2023)?[43]

First, losses. Second, consistently so year after year since its foundation. Third, the trend was to worsen. Fourth, results were far worse than direct competitors (e.g., Apple Music). And fifth, that even in opposition to other streaming companies such as Netflix or similar ones such as Canva.

Table 4 shows that since its start,[44] Spotify always accumulated losses without exception and without any signs of improvement. If we assume a two-year lag time between policies and results, and therefore we consider the year of 2023 still influenced by the first period actions (ended in 1/1/2022), in the six years from 2018 to 2023, losses amounted to 1.8 billion euros.

Also, the negative results were not shared by direct competitors or other streaming and alike companies but seemed to be specific to Spotify: In 2023, Apple Services (which include Apple Music plus iCloud,

---

[42]Contrary to several reports of an upward trend for **film** and **TV** piracy.

[43]As mentioned, the cut-point before and after new policies were introduced is the start of 2022, being reasonable to consider around a 2-year lag time.

[44]As referred, born in 2006, Spotify launched its platform into the market in 2008.

Table 4 Spotify's net income (bottom line)

Year	Profits/losses (million euros)
2009	−18.8
2010	−28.5
2011	−45.4
2012	−83.6
2013	−63
2014	−188
2015	−230
2016	−539
2017	−1,235
2018	−78
2019	−186
2020	−581
2021	−34
2022	−430
2023	−532

2024	+1,138

Source: Spotify's annual reports; Statista

App Store, and Apple TV)[45] had 2.6 times the gross margin of Spotify (+71 percent against 27 percent).

And Spotify's results were far behind than those of other streaming services at the end of 2021: Its operating margin (Ebit)[46] was 94 million euros against $6.2 billion for Netflix, and Netflix, contrary to Spotify (except for the first five years of 1998–2002), has constantly been profitable and increasingly so (net profits of $5 billion in 2021 and 2022 and of $5.4 billion in 2023).

---

[45] There is no individual data for Apple Music and, thus, the inference from Apple Services, all together.

[46] Sales minus variable costs (cost of goods sold) = gross margin.

   After deducting fixed costs one obtains the net margin (Ebitda).

   Less depreciation and amortization equals to operational margin/income (Ebit).

   Then taking out interests and taxes, one finally reaches the bottom line (net profit).

A lookalike service is Canva,[47] which is a graphic platform. It also offers clients the two options of free and paying. However, results differ strongly: Canva, which started in 2012, has been profitable year after year since 2017.

So, the question is **why?** Why the dismal profitability of Spotify?

And the answer is that **both** Spotify's **business model** and **tactics** had (1) *several* and (2) *serious* flaws, with both starting in 2022 being increasingly corrected with the consequence of a positive Ebit (earnings before interest and taxes) in the third quarter of 2023 (32 million euros) and then the first full year ever of net profits, positive bottom line, in 2024 (1.1 billion euros).

This chapter will concentrate on the business model changes and **Chapter 6** later on how tactical modifications also improved Spotify's performance.[48]

---

[47]Canva is a graphic design platform that allows users to create a wide range of visual content, such as graphics, presentations, posters, or other digital designs. It provides tools to help users design, without having advanced graphic design skills.

Thus, in rigor it is not a streaming service; it is a digital platform that delivers media content such as music, movies, live events, TV shows, and so on over the Internet in real-time, allowing users to consume the content without the need to download it beforehand, as Netflix, Spotify, and YouTube.

[48]Strategy's modifications also played a role, although a minor one, namely with the expansion of the offer into more regions of both podcasts and audiobooks in terms of titles and languages. That will be addressed together with tactics in Chapter 6.

All together that explains Spotify's turnaround after near two decades (2006–2023) of continuous losses since:

1. If its theory of business was sound (as per the main text above), problems must be found elsewhere. In the present case, as it happens with
2. The business model; and
3. Tactics (the functional areas of marketing, finance, operations, human resources management, etc.). And to a lesser degree with:
4. The strategy (choice of geographical areas, industries, and segments).

Since and again as per Figure 1 of Page 3:

Company performance	
Design	Implementation
Theory of Business	Strategy (geographical areas, industries, and segments)
Business Model	Tactics (functional areas: marketing, human resources management, finance, etc.)

MUSIC STREAMING COMPANIES			
Company	**Platform (for other purchases)**	**Free (but with ads) option**	**Pay option**
Spotify	No	Yes	Yes
Apple Music	Yes	No	Yes
Amazon Music	Yes	Yes	Yes
YouTube Music	Yes	Yes	Yes
Napster	No	No	Yes
Tidal	No	No	Yes

Figure 13 The basic pillars of the business model of music streaming companies

To find the weaknesses of Spotify business model, one must start by **defining it** as it was until the beginning of 2022 (the first period under analysis at present).

Figure 13 compares the **fundamental pillars** of the business models of music streaming companies: Spotify (1) had no platform (contrary to Apple, YouTube, or Amazon) and offered the options of (2) free and (3) paying (like YouTube and Amazon), but not Apple, Napster, or Tidal.[49]

From the above table one fact seems a *false problem* and *two really stand out*.

The *nonproblem* is Spotify's offering a *free option*. First because of the absence of a platform (a surface where other valences can be bought like

---

[49]Within premium four sub-options were created: (1) individual, (2) two persons, (3) family (up to six persons), and (4) student.

The latter three options came out cheaper for each person than the first option.

Apple had the very same sub-options than Spotify and with the very same prices with the exceptions of the option for two persons that did not exist.

Since the option for two persons came out cheaper for each person than the individual option, that meant that overall, in average, Spotify's prices were slightly lower than Apple Music.

How much lower depends on the percentage of clients choosing the two-person option.

films, books, phone services, etc. and by default music) such as that of YouTube and so on to attract new clients. Second, because other very profitable streaming and alike companies (e.g., Canva) were offering (not only temporary but also permanent) free options and remained always very profitable.

There was, however, a major difference between Canva and Spotify.

In spite of Canva offering the free option, only **one-third** of its users selected it (with **two-thirds** preferring to pay), but, in the instance of Spotify, the percentage of clients opting for paying was solely **44 percent** against **56 percent** (in 2021) choosing the free one.

The reason why a minority of Spotify clients opted for the pay/premium option was obvious enough: They **didn't** think that it was worthwhile, that the added value compensated the price. And that although Spotify was underpricing Canva (a lot) and its direct competitors (Apple Music, etc.) somewhat.[50]

---

[50]When a business offers a free (but with ads as in the case of Spotify) and a paying option, most profits are expected to come from the latter, not the former. Otherwise, why have the latter if it cannibalizes the former?

Thus a free option, even if (because of the ads) it generates a profit, it must still serve (also) to attract users first and then induce them to become paying clients.

In short, the free option does not exist for itself, but as a means for a larger profit center (the premium option) and, thus, the importance of great differences in value among them.

But in the case of Spotify, there is a second reason: Royalties are paid every time a music track is played, be it by a free or paying user.

And the available information is that the revenue generated by ads is not enough to cover the cost of royalties.

Therefore, the free option is not a smaller profit center than the paying option. The free option is a loss center.

And from that follows the further need to incentivize users to transfer from one to the other.

Something to be done by adding value to the pay option and not by reducing value to the free one; otherwise, one will decrease its attractive power regarding pirate sites and other competitors and, therefore, its usefulness.

But then there was a *second weakness* in Spotify's business model: Contrary to some competitors such as Amazon Music, Apple Music, and YouTube Music, it did not benefit from an already existing **platform** created for other purposes (movies, books, etc.).

Indeed, in the previous Figure 13, Spotify is the **sole** company that, while offering both free and pay options, has no platform: Both Amazon Music and YouTube Music have, while Apple Music has a platform but no free option, and Napster and Tidal operate neither a platform nor a free option.

3.2.2. The Second Period of Spotify: From the Early 2022 Onwards

What Spotify did starting in 2022 was to address the above **two** weaknesses. First, increasing the difference in value between the free and pay options. And second, obtaining a platform.

And in order to augment the benefits of the pay option, Spotify acted upon **two** fronts:

- Improving the quality of **present services** through both:
  - *Artificial intelligence* and *Management tools*, and
- Introducing **new major services**, namely audiobooks, karaoke, and music videos.

Since according to CEO Daniel Ek *"everything we're doing can be augmented creating a much stronger value proposition for our consumers with the help of* **AI** *and that makes me the most excited since starting the platform 20 years ago,"* Spotify invested heavily in **AI** driving *small service changes* that made the platform more user-friendly with, for example, automating better playlists, fueling more personal recommendations and the smart shuffle: a feature that mixes up playlists offering a more dynamic listening experience by introducing new tracks aligned with user preferences.

Then followed other improvements, still incremental in nature, but now *of greater magnitude* such as the introduction of a sleep timer allowing to set a timer to stop music after a certain duration (ideal for those who enjoy listening to music before sleeping), or group sessions that enable real-time listening experiences for multiple users, or still collaborative playlists (facilitating collective music curation and playlists sharing with friends).

And *podcasts* were another area where the impact of AI was felt most specially as algorithms leveraged the match between listeners and podcasts or real-time transcriptions.

Still other podcasts enhancements were due not to AI, but to *other management tools*.

Although podcasts were introduced in 2015, recent years saw significant increases in their quality through:

- The *acquisition of several companies* like Gimlet Media, Anchor, and Parcast which allowed Spotify to produce its own content;
- *Exclusive deals with popular hosts* such as Joe Rogan (the Joe Rogan experience);
- Several *innovative policies* (ad-free podcast subscriptions where Spotify shared revenue with creators) and *innovations* (video podcasts); and
- The *abandonment* of less successful projects such as the deal with Harry and Meghan (the Duke and Duchess of Sussex) that during 2.5 years cost $25 million.

"*The end result was that while a drag in 2023, in 2024 podcasts became a profit center for us*" (CEO Daniel Ek).

Then premium users benefited still from **major innovations**, that is, important **new services** introduced for the first time:

- *Karaoke* (in 6/2022);
- *Audiobooks* (9/2022); and
- *Music videos* (3/2024).

Karaoke, a feature that the major competitor Apple Music had been offering for long, now allows Spotify clients not only to sing their favorite tracks with real-time lyrics, but also receive performance scores based on vocal accuracy.

The *audiobooks* catalogs in the hundreds of thousands of titles are both accessible to premium users (15 hours free per month) or can be purchased individually.[51]

And *music videos* were first offered in March 2024 across 12 markets and then later expanded in October to 85 additional ones, bringing the total to 97.

The above summarizes how Spotify increased the difference in value offer between free (with ads) and pay (premium) users. And that was **one of the major faults of its business model**.

But, as per previous Figure 13 in Page 53, there was a **second flaw**, namely the **absence of a platform**, contrary to Apple Music, Amazon Music, or YouTube Music, all having surfaces where other things are being sold: from phone services to books, to films.

That was addressed starting at the beginning of the year of 2024 by increasingly consolidating Spotify's presence in the *Apple platform*.

Indeed, although Spotify had access to iOS (iPhone operating system)[52] through the App Store since 2009, a major legal victory in early 2024 (which included a $2 billion fine under an antitrust ruling) significantly increased Spotify's access to iPhone users because of:

1. *Pricing information display*: The legal victory enables Spotify to share all price information for its streaming plans directly within its

---

[51]If a premium user exhausts the monthly application, the top-up hours option then allows to purchase additional listening hours with a 12-month validity.

[52]iOS (iPhone operating system), which is the proprietary mobile operating system developed by Apple specifically for its mobile devices, and Android are the two dominant mobile operating systems in the global smartphone market (with 28 percent and 72 percent of market share, respectively).

iOS app in the European Union (formerly Apple's rules prevented Spotify from informing about subscription prices and promotions inside the App); and

2. *Other information* as well: Spotify can since then inform iOS users that all types of Apple's commission fees can be avoided through direct purchases on Spotify's website.

And so, together, with the ability to display information both about pricing and the external purchase options, they structurally strengthened Apple phones as a platform for Spotify users, with the consequence that Spotify App has been downloaded or updated 120 billion times on Apple devices and became one of the most popular music streaming apps on the App Store.

The importance of Apple as a platform is demonstrated by the fact that in spite of Spotify's March 2024 legal victory, it continued to push for additional rights such as the ability to offer direct in app purchases without Apple's fees.

Figure 14 summarizes the business model changes undertaken by Spotify since the start of 2022 in (1) enlarging its access to a *platform*,

Objective	How		
To have a **platform**	Legal victory allowing for greater access for **Apple** users through iOS app available in the App Store		
Increase the **difference in value** between premium (pay) and free (with ads) options	Improvements in the **quality of present** services through	**Artificial intelligence**	
		Management tools	**Acquisition** of companies (content suppliers)
			Exclusive agreements with top performers
			Planned abandonment of underperformers
	Introducing major **new services**	*Audiobooks*	
		Karaoke	
		Music videos	

Figure 14 Spotify business model changes (2022–2024)

(2) improving the *quality* of present services, and (3) adding *new* services to the premium (pay) option.

The consequent improvements of Spotify's business model impacted on financial results: a positive operating income (ebit) in the third quarter of 2023, as well as in all 2024 quarters (+168, +266, +454, +477), and a first full year of profits (bottom line) in 2024 (1.1 billion euros). The market value (market capitalization) in the first quarter of 2022 was at 29 billion euros and reached 90 billion euros by the end of 2024.

And this illustrates that a **sound business model** is either a necessary condition or at the very least always a quite strong facilitator for performance, thus requiring constant attention for improvement (see appendix in the next page).

And for that, sometimes changing a *single pillar* is enough. *McDonald's* is an example[53].

---

[53]The autobiography of Ray Kroc (Grinding It Out) and the classic McDonald's: Behind the Arches by John F. Love are excellent sources for further details. The movie The Founder provides a brief summary.

Appendix

As Chapter 6 will analyze, in the case of Spotify strategic changes were minor, but in tactics they were major.

Thus comes the question—**how important for Spotify turnaround were business model reforms** as **compared** to those performed on **tactics**?

Sure that business model modifications were **large**, but what is the evidence that they definitely played a role in making Spotify profitable?

The answer requires following a sequence of steps.

First of all, profitability is dependent on *three* broad categories of variables:

  a. Number of *clients;*
  b. *Margin* that each one brings (price minus direct costs); and
  c. Level of *fixed costs.*

Chapter 6 will later indicate how tactics addressed B and C. For instance, how price increases impacted on B and layoffs on C (areas of marketing and human resources management, respectively).

Second, the *number of clients* (A) depends on the theory of business (market growth) and the business model, whose role is to change users from the free option to the paying one and, thus, transforming clients' value into company value. In scheme:

Cause / Impact on clients	Theory of business	Business model
Free (ads)	✓	
Paying (premium)	✓	✓

As a consequence (and **third**) whatever impact the business model changes had, they should be visible in terms of the *number of paying (premium) clients*.

The **table** below presents for the last decade (2015–2024) Spotify's number of total users and the subgroup of paying clients. The line in bold stresses that major business model reforms were implemented since the start of 2022.

Year \ Type of users	Total users (in millions)	Percentage of increase of total users over the previous year	Paying/ premium users (in millions)	Percentage of increase of paying/ premium users regarding previous year	Percentage of paying users over total users
2015	91	–	28	–	31%
2016	123	35%	48	71%	39%
2017	160	30%	71	48%	44%
2018	207	29%	96	35%	46%
2019	271	31%	124	29%	46%
2020	345	27%	155	25%	45%
2021	406	18%	180	16%	44%
2022	489	20%	205	14%	42%
2023	602	23%	236	15%	39%
2024	675	12%	263	11%	39%

(Cut point indicated between 2021 and 2022)

And from the table, the major inferences are:

- Both the total number of users and paying users always increased in *absolute* terms year after year;
- But both at a *decreasing rate*;
- In the *beginning*, the yearly increase in paying was larger than the augment in total (years 2016–2018), but then
- The relationship reversed until 2024 when the increase in the proportion of paying users was **almost the same** as total users

(11 percent against 12 percent), marking the first time that was the case since 2018;

- As a consequence, the percentage of paying clients regarding the total number of users which had been decreasing since then **stabilized** at 39 percent (bottom line of right-side column).

In sum, the **year of 2024** saw (1) not only an **increase** in the number of **premium** clients but also (2) at a **similar rate** than the **total** number of users and (3) large enough to **stabilize** the percentage of the former in the latter, which (4) had been continuously **diminishing** in the previous years. All of these indicate a positive impact of the business model reforms initiated in 2022 and enhanced henceforth, if one considers as one should a lag time effect of the policies changes.

3.3. McDonald's: The Importance of a Single Change

McDonald's is an example of how sometimes **changing a single pillar** of the business model is the **difference** between bankruptcy and becoming the Number 1 franchising company in the world,[54] valued at 215 billion, and with its brand worth ranking fifth: after Apple, Google, Microsoft, and Amazon. The company is present in over 100 countries with more than 40,000 outlets.

Founded in 1940 by the McDonald (Richard and Maurice) brothers and expanded through franchising by Ray Kroc, McDonald's owns its success to none of the above, but to **Harry Sonneborn**, a financial consultant, who introduced a single change in the business model that opened the path to prosperity.

It all started when the McDonald brothers created an extremely successful restaurant with clients absolutely flocking under the following theory of business:

First and foremost, **fast service** as order to service took an average of 15 seconds and a consequence of (1) *specialization* (every 1 of the 12 employees repeated endlessly the same very narrow task), (2) *standardization* of procedures (in time, components[55] and actions for preparing the hamburgers, French fries, and milkshakes), and (3) a *layout* that minimized movements after having been studied by drawing with chalk several versions in the flour of a tennis court.

All that allowed service in *15 seconds* even as preassembled food waited for clients to reach the counter.

Second, low prices, as a consequence of selling only the *three products* of burgers, French fries, and milkshakes, and *economies of scale* (quantity discounts from suppliers) and *benefits of experience.*

---

[54]Henceforth and unless referred otherwise always 2023 data.
[55]All hamburgers were served with ketchup, mustard, onions, and two pickles, and any clients who wanted food prepared differently would have to wait. That is, the rule to enforce standardization was to have it *our way.*

What, on its turn, impacted on the **third** cornerstone, namely the satisfactory **quality** of the food: repetitiously served it allowed for continuous improvement.[56]

And finally, there were two accessory factors: *small real estate construction space* since clients would eat outside the restaurant, and, *cleanliness*, a consequence of the *practicality* of dispensing with all dishware and cutlery with clients using their hands and disposing of the paper and cardboard packaging. That also helped to keep costs at a minimum.

The clients' answer to the theory of business (*speed, low price, quality in three products,* and *cleanliness and practicality*) was overwhelming: They flocked to the restaurant, and so in 1954 Ray Kroc, a milkshake machines salesman, was attracted to the restaurant to investigate the reasons for the large orders and ended up signing a contract to replicate S. Bernardino's restaurant by franchising.[57]

Since Kroc believed that the S. Bernardino restaurant was scalable, his objective was to clone it in other U.S. locations. Thus, the **theory of business** for each additional restaurant was basically the **same**. No difference here, regarding that of the founding brothers.

Ray Kroc's motto was **Quality, Service, Cleanliness, and Value** (QSC&V). These four words became the cornerstone of McDonald's.

However, since *franchising was built as a specific operation*, the **business model** was different as characterized by **three tenets**:

1. The McDonald brothers retained all rights of *authorizing* any changes in how the franchisees worked;
2. The franchisees had to *abide* by the rules; and

---

[56]At the beginning, the McDonald brothers experimented with other products such as barbecues only to abandon them.
[57]Initial franchising attempts by the brothers in California and Arizona had met with failure as they struggled to enforce absolute replication.

3. For each new franchise, Kroc received a *$950* franchise fee and *1.9 percent* of the restaurants revenues,[58] of which he would remit *0.5 percent* to the brothers.

And **in the two years** to follow, Kroc's enthusiasm would translate into nine franchisees openings (where again clients would line up to be served) and… near bankruptcy on top of major problems.

The problems were the hassle to enforce compliance on franchisees, starting with the menu and ending with the procedures. And the near bankruptcy a mere consequence that 1.4 percent of a 15¢ hamburger was far insufficient to build a franchising company upon.

Then comes Harry Sonneborn, a financial consultant, who introduced a single change in the business model: **the land**, which fell outside the agreement between Kroc and the McDonald brothers since it takes into account only everything that happened **inside** each restaurant and not how the business was structured. Thus, a separate real estate company called Franchise Realty Corporation was created to deal with the land.

Instead of letting the franchisee select the place and then buy the land usually with a bank loan, McDonald's would itself control the land starting by selecting the site.[59]

Initially, the land deal was called "*top lease*": Under the arrangement, the landowner obtained a mortgage and built a (then) $40,000 McDonald's on the property and leased it to McDonald's for 20 years for nearly

---

[58]A hamburger at the time cost 15 ¢.

[59]A critical task exemplified by what happened when General Foods bought Burger Chef: It eliminated the 54 men field staff who scouted for new properties and supervised new store development. As they had higher salaries than the General Foods managers dispatched to run the chain… they were replaced by independent real estate brokers whose property proposals were ill-suited for fast-food. The outcome was General Foods being forced within a short time to halt its new store development and taking in 1971 a $75 million write-off on its fast-food operations.

$700 a month, that would on its turn lease it back to the franchisees at a 20 percent markup.

Later to the policy of leasing both the property and the building from the landowner, McDonald's added the alternative of owning both the land and the building financed with mortgages from banks.

And in the few instances that a franchisee owned the land already, it would be leased to McDonald's that would then sublease it back.

Control of the land, although a *single issue*, **completely changed** the business model of Kroc's franchising company. First in greater control over the franchisees due to the lease of land.

Second, **revenues** increased sharply, not only because of the initial 20 percent and later 40 percent markup on the leases, but also because a percentage rent would also be due kicking in a 5 percent of sales over a certain level.

Third, there was the **quality of franchisees** attracted. Kroc wanted them to have *entrepreneurial spirit*, not wealthy people who would frequently end up being absentee managers.

Since the potential entrepreneurs frequently did not have the funds or bank credit neither for the land nor for constructing the building, McDonald's intermediation would solve the issue.

Finally, the valorization with time of the land both of franchises and restaurants directly created and exploited by Kroc's firm would serve as guarantees for new loans to further **expand** the business.

When Kroc entered into the contract with the brothers (in 1954), there was San Bernardino's and other **10** problematic (for not abiding by the rules) franchisees. When Kroc introduced the land clause change (in 1956) there were **19** restaurants.

Henceforth: 40 (in 1957), 145 (in 1959), 228 (1960), 1,500 (1970), 6,200 (1980), 7,500 (1984) until the 40,000 of today (2023).

Figure 15 summarizes this section. It is a synthesis and thus leaves out several other factors: In 1961, Kroc bought out the McDonald brothers by *2.7 million* (worth ± 27.7 million in 2023), which gave Kroc the rights to specify how McDonald's restaurants would operate, as well as the name; the eventual handshake agreement (?) on *1 percent* of all McDonald's revenues, which Kroc refused to acknowledge and never paid; Kroc opened a McDonald's restaurant *in front* of the now-renamed original one as Big M of the brothers, leading them into bankruptcy by the end of the decade and what constitutes an example of the power of image and branding (to no avail, the brothers advertised to the locals that theirs was the original restaurant that had been located in the same place for three decades), and so on.

Although the above are also interesting aspects of the McDonald's story, **the essential**, however, is a different fact: The theory of business was valid and innovative, but Kroc courted bankruptcy.

Theory of business		Business model of franchising company	
San Bernardino restaurant	Franchisees	Under **Kroc**	With **Sonneborn**
1. **Fast** service (15 seconds)		1. **Rules** set by McDonald brothers	
2. Only **three** products: hamburgers, french fries, and milkshakes		2. Franchisees must **abide** by the rules	
3. Satisfactory food **quality**		3. Fees of **$950** per franchise and **1.9%** in revenues of which **0.5%** to be remitted to the brothers	
4. **Small** real estate space (clients eat outside)			4. **Land controlled** by Kroc and leased at **40%** markup to the franchisees (on top of **5%** rent on revenues)
5. **Clean** and **practical** (no dishware)			

Figure 15 McDonald's: theory of business and business model

The solution was **a single** change in the business model, which transformed near receivership into the most valuable franchising operation in the world.[60]

Summing up, **Spotify** in the former section exemplified how a **few** (two) flaws in a business model can prevent performance, and **McDonald's** now illustrates how sometimes **one** single change will make all the difference. It is useful nevertheless to look at other instances where **multiple** alterations are needed.

3.4. SolarCity: Performing Several Modifications to Have a Sound Business Model

When SolarCity[61] was created in 2006 the solar panel industry was **struggling**.[62]

That, in spite of the fact that there was a potential *demand*, from genuinely environmentally concerned customers, and from others who did so for the sake of image.

Also *supply* was becoming increasingly available with technology improvements translated into an ever-growing number of devices to store and utilize the immense potential of energy provided by the sun: *one hour of sunshine equals one year of earth's consumption.*

And government *subsidies*, both to consumers and producers, made the industry increasingly attractive.

Thus, all the above constituted the cornerstones upon which a **sound business theory** could be built (first column in Figure 16).

---

[60]Even today, McDonald's remains different from other franchises in that it owns 45 percent of the land on which its restaurants sit and 70 percent of the buildings. The rest it leases directly from the seller (the so-called contract for deed) or with a bank loan. All franchisees pay rent to McDonald's on a monthly set amount, or percent of revenue.

[61]Later in 2016 incorporated into Tesla as Tesla Energy.

[62]Henceforth, whenever written, solar panel(s) refers to solar panel and other sun energy devices such as linear concentrator systems (u-shaped mirrors), mirrored dishes, power tower systems, and other instruments to collect the sun's energy.

SOLARCITY (TESLA ENERGY)

	Theory of business	Problems	Business model
Demand exists due to customers	Genuinely environmental concerned	Upfront investment	Lease / Chinese / Large own factory / New technology / Decrease in cost impacting on price due to — B2C→B2B; Sales — Marketing, Price constant, Effective promotion below line (Twitter, etc.)
	Status symbol		
Supply exists	One hour sunshine equal one year earth consumption	Risk	Software for sunshine level evaluation / Contract — Ended if house sold, Maintenance + monitoring, Option of more efficient panels, Storage batteries
	Technological improvements		
Rentability	Government subsidies to — Consumers / Producers	Cumbersome	Global service
		Ugly	Solar roofs and other structure fitting devices

Figure 16 Solarcity (Tesla Energy)

Nevertheless, several major **problems** remained preventing businesses profitability (second column in Figure 16).

First of all, the *upfront investment.* All industry players were expecting the price of solar panels to decrease, but *no one was taking ownership of the problem.*

On top of that, the product was perceived as *risky* with the consumer unsure if the house received enough sunshine. Procrastination was then further incentivized by constant technological improvements that created the belief that "next year's models will surely be more efficient...."

Still the use of solar panels was *cumbersome* as companies that sold them did not install them, requiring customers to be proactive.

And on top of it all, solar panels were *ugly*, not fitting the house structure (Figure 16).

So how was it possible for SolarCity to become (1) within seven years the leading residential solar installer in the United States, (2) the Number 2 overall installation company, including for industrial clients; (3) a company with one-third of the market share when acquired by Tesla (in 2016 and renamed Tesla Energy), (4) at the price of $2.6 billion; (5) a company that had until then posted year-after-year positive gross profits; and (6) a company that become percentage-wise more profitable than Tesla Auto itself ($1.1 billion gross profit in 2023)? How come?

The answer is by constructing a **business model** that *addressing the major problems facing the industry,* removed the *obstacles* that prevented the theory of business from becoming *fully practical.*

And such a business model had **four pillars.**

The *upfront investment* was diminished by leasing, instead of selling the equipment.

The no-money-down policy (including the option of a $0 down agreement with SolarCity owning the equipment) led to an immediate jump in sales and, thus, larger orders to suppliers (then mostly Chinese) and, consequently, scale economies, and lower costs and prices.

Then, when SolarCity reached 110,000 customers, it opted for *in-house production* and built the largest factory in the Western hemisphere using the most efficient technology (18.5 percent efficient at turning the sunlight into energy, compared to 14.5 percent of the technology used by competition).

Sales were also increased through *three other items*: adding *B2B to B2C* using wholesalers such as Walmart and direct sales to corporations such as Intel; keeping contract prices *constant* by opposition to the yearly increases of most utilities; and a below-the-line[63] (low-cost) effective *promotion*: Elon Musk would tweet to his (then) 80 million followers every time a new feature was added to products, together with presentations and press releases.

Then the client-*perceived risk* was decreased by (1) evaluating with a software before providing the service if the house received enough sunshine, (2) adding and enforcing a clause in the contract that the contract could be terminated when/if the house was sold, (3) offering both monitoring and maintenance as part of the contract, (4) making available storage batteries manufactured by Tesla, and (5) providing the option of renewing the contract with more efficient panels.

Last, the *ugliness* problem was solved with solar roofs that did not stand out but fitted the house structure, and global service made SolarCity far less *cumbersome* as it offered an all-inclusive package: evaluation of the level of sunshine reaching the house; several product alternatives of installation; financing and leasing options; and monitoring, maintenance, as well as repairs and energy storage solutions. Industrial clients could also benefit from consultancy for large projects.

---

[63]Promotion is divided between *above the line* when one pays for space or time (e.g., outdoors or TV ads) and *below the line* when that does not occur (tweets, communities, press releases, etc.)

These characteristics of the business model that addressed the major problems that were preventing the theory of business from reaching its potential guaranteed SolarCity *survival* until the Chinese flooded the market with solar panels making prices collapse.

In part this was due to increasing demand from SolarCity and competitors and the other part was a consequence of the Chinese industrial policy of targeting high-potential businesses, through incentives to enable low price which would end up creating the demand.

Finally, SolarCity profitability further increased after its merger with Tesla, as a consequence of several **synergies**.

SolarCity makes solar panels. Tesla manufactures electric cars and storage batteries. The latter placed in households can charge both cars and solar panels. Clients who buy all together benefit from global service.

And so was created an integrated sustainable energy company supplying end-to-end clean energy solutions.

Synergies were so strong that **E. Musk** said that *it was an accident of history that the two companies (SolarCity and Tesla) were ever built as separate entities.*

3.5. Conclusion

The examples provided in this chapter stress upon three aspects of a business model.

The case of **Spotify** illustrated that though a sound business model does not by itself guarantee performance (a good theory of business is also required), a bad business model (even with a solid theory of business) prevents performance optimization. Thus, a well-designed business model is always a *necessary condition* for excellence. Indispensable.[64]

---

[64]And at the very least a, very, very, strong enabler of survival.

And such a business model should have *two qualities*. First, address the *problems* that hamper the theory of business from materializing its full potential. That was illustrated by **SolarCity**.

And then *maximize value* for the company while creating value for the customers—to add the former to the latter, as exemplified by **McDonald's**.

Thus, the examples of this chapter and of the previous one indicate that **both** a sound business model and a good theory of business are **necessary** for outstanding performance.

But in a world of constant change, **how best to update them?** And with which **frequency?**

Those are the tasks of the **next two chapters**, before we conclude.

CHAPTER 4

Why, How, and *When* to Review the Theory of Business

If we keep on doing what worked in the past,
we are going to fail.
(Peter Drucker)

4.1. Why to Review the Theory of Business

There are two reasons. The lesson of *Abraham Lincoln's* anecdote and *unexpected successes*.

4.1.1. Abraham Lincoln

His election for president culminated a long list of failures[65] as shop owner, postmaster, land officer (application rejected), as well as defeats in elections both for the Congress and the Senate.

So when Lincoln friends were exultant with his presidential election, he told them the story of the king, who, after asking his sages what was the **only thing constant in life**, received the answer: **change**. As noted along *History* by scientists (Heraclitus), religious leaders (Buddha), poets (Camões), and emperors (Marcus Aurelius).

With time, everything changes, be it demographics, economics, culture, or technology.

But frequently when a company gets into trouble, one thinks that the causes are internal, when the real cause often is that reality assumptions do not hold anymore.

When reality changes, the theory of business must change with it.

Let's look at **three** cases selected for being **quite far apart** in time: one from the beginning of the twentieth century; another, at the start of this one; and a third, of the present decade.

Following World War I, **Sears Roebuck** focused on being the supplier of the American farmer, based on two assumptions:

1. The American farmer was *isolated*; and
2. It had *different needs* from both suburban and urban consumers.

---

[65]Reminding W. Churchill's observation that success is going from failure to failure without ever stopping.

From such a **theory of business**, followed the **business model**: (1) *a mail catalog*, (2) *a guarantee of* money back and no questions asked, (3) a network of *specialized suppliers*, and, finally (4) *a mail order plant* large enough to operate great quantities of goods cheaply and quickly.

However, within a few years (in the 1920s) the Ford Motor Co. revolution decreased sharply the price of automobiles. That, on top of significant improvements in public transportation, made no longer true the assumption regarding the isolation of the American farmer, which required Sears to realign with reality by being the buyer of the suburban middle-class family.

As a consequence, Sears became a *brick and mortar company* in direct competition with Marks & Spencer and other large retailers.

Another example, now from the *beginning of this century* is **IBM**, under the narrative of its CEO L. Gerstner in his 2002 book: Who Says Elephants Can't Dance?

Moore's law (the power of microchips double every two years) and the increasing strength of software made that the best common way to process information was no longer mainframes, but network computer systems.[66]

That required **three** new core competences for IBM: (1) *software* and (2) *service binding* a (3) *constellation* of hardware composed by mainframes, minicomputers, PCs, stations, network interface cards, nodes, switches, routers, and others.

As a result of these changes introduced by Gerstner from 1993 until his retirement in 2002, IBM market capitalization rose from $29 billion to $168 billion, in spite of the technological changes brought into the industry forefront by other players such as Microsoft, Apple, and Intel.

---

[66]Special cases aside, such as research centers still requiring super or mini-supercomputers.

Those changes were irreversible. The decline of IBM was not, provided the company changed its reality assumptions and adapted to them. And that is what IBM did under L. Gerstner's leadership.

He saw that the telecommunications industry was about to undergo dramatic changes with the network model of computing replacing the (then) PC-dominated world. Henceforth, the work would not be revolving around PCs, but these would be just one of the components connected to a network of many devices creating a huge demand for computing infrastructure. The core task of IBM was to build that. And, thus, IBM's network business was born.

A further example, now of the *present decade*, is provided by **Gorillas**.

Born in May 2020, it became a unicorn in just nine months with a **business theory based on**:

1. In the center of the COVID-19 pandemic, many people worked from home and *refrained from personal contacts*, even when they were not expressly forced to by government-imposed shutdowns;
2. *Fresh products* (fruit, meat) were deemed more important for in-store purchases than more standardized ones such as groceries (rice, pasta); and
3. A *rapid delivery* of these fresh products (bread, cheese, milk, eggs) was frequently needed.

Thus, the **business model** of Gorillas was to *home-deliver groceries in 10 minutes* operating from warehouses spread out in European and American cities, charging a markup price and a delivery fee.

During its life, Gorillas achieved **three records**. The fastest-ever company to become an unicorn: only nine months. Raised $3 billion in less than a year-and-a-half's time: May 2020 to September 2021. And the fastest unicorn to go out of business: In little over 2.5 years, from May 2020 to December 2022, becoming cash-strapped, it was acquired by Getir for $1.2 billion.

The reason being that as the COVID-19 pandemic subsided, the theory of business *assumptions ceased to be valid*, with people allowing themselves more time to buy food outside their homes and, thus, increasingly unwilling to pay the markup prices and fees for instant (10 minutes) home delivery.

It is also illustrative that within the food delivery business, the companies *most directly hit* by the end of the COVID-19 pandemic were those based on (1) *speed* and (2) *standardized products*.

So many direct and indirect competitors (those including a larger choice of foods than Gorillas) disappeared, were bought, or are at present struggling due to large negative results: Buyk, Jokr, Fridge No More, GoPuff, Homegrocer, Peapod, and FreshDirect.

By opposition, *surviving and thriving* are those *picking up from third parties* stores, including restaurants (e.g., Uber Eats) and those that deliver great *value addition* such as pre-prepared meals (e.g., Gousto).

In short, the cases of Sears Roebuck, IBM, and Gorillas (selected for being quite far apart in time) illustrate that as reality changes so must the theory of business so that both remain aligned. As reality evolves, the theory of business must change with it.

But there is another major reason to review the theory of business: **unexpected successes.**[67]

---

[67]There are a few very rare instances of a third reason to review the theory of business: mission (a concept introduced in the appendix of Chapter 1 in Page 5) accomplished, the organization purpose is fulfilled.

At the beginning of the twentieth century, **ATT** became a giant based on four simple observations: (1) *few* homes had fixed phones (most were in street, post offices, and public spaces), (2) *all* households wanted them if (3) supplied at *low* prices, what could be done due to (4) *large* economies of scale mostly in infrastructure.

So, a phone in every home became ATT's mission, whose feasibility was demonstrated by the fact that little over two decades it was near completion with 94 percent of the U.S. area under coverage, ATT constituting a monopoly (which federal law later forced to break up into smaller firms—the so-called baby bells—to foster competition) and the original ATT (re)defining its mission to include international communications.

These cases of *mission accomplished* are, however, very rare. Mostly, the need to redefine the business comes from (environmental) change or unexpected successes.

4.1.2. Unexpected Successes

The importance of looking at unexpected successes is exemplified by **how IBM reacted to Apple's PCs.**

Until then it was assumed that the best common way to process information was through mainframes.

Moore's law (chips power doubling every two years) and the software revolution made that increasingly obsolete.

At first IBM, not realizing the above, ignored the PC market only for a couple of years later, faced with Apple's success, to recognize the change and launch its own version of PCs, at a discount, supported by a strong promotion campaign and cloning the distribution channels and sales organization of Apple.[68]

---

[68]The recent history of IBM is a carousel of **five** major ups and downs.

First, it overtook Remington Rand (Univac), ATT, GE, Olivetti, Bull, and so on and achieved such a large market share that the industry became known as the snow white and the seven dwarfs which complained that IBM was *not competition,* but *the environment:* They waited for IBM to launch a new model and then would come up with a copy at a lower price.

IBM's source of success was the realization that the restraint on information processing of mainframes and minicomputers was not in hardware, but in *software and service,* both areas where IBM excelled.

A second phase came with the introduction of *PCs* by Apple demonstrating that the reality assumption that information processing had to come from mainframes was obsolete.

After a period of hesitation, IBM reacted strongly and with success replicating Apple's distribution channels and sales force, and multiplying Apple's budget of advertising, public relations, and sales promotion on top of offering considerable price discounts.

A third phase started when IBM became complacent with its success in the PCs segment and made the wrong assumptions: one *managerial* and another *technological.*

IBM assumed that its motto and advertising slogan "no one has ever been fired for hiring IBM" applied also to lower-cost PCs (where it made far less sense) and even to those purchased for home use (where it made even less sense).

And the technological myth was that the PC's information capacity would remain limited and, consequently, sales would not boom. Moore's law and software progress destroyed that.

(continues in the next page)

Another illustration comes from the **vehicles industry**.

When Alfred Sloan became the chairman of **General Motors,** he introduced segmentation based on the *vehicle purpose* (for professional or for personal use), then dividing the former in *specific categories* (urban transportation, long-distance transportation, construction and related, etc.), and the latter in terms of income: *"a car for every purse."*

And thus distinguishing among brands in terms of *price ranges*: Chevrolet, Pontiac, Buick, Cadillac, and so on.

In the forthcoming years, General Motors maintained its segmentation criteria (although sometimes the price ranges of brands would overlap creating cannibalism) until **Chrysler** had two great successes with *SUVs*—sports utility vehicles—and minivans.

And **General Motors** also had an unexpected success far exceeding its most optimistic expectations with *light trucks*.

That signaled that vehicles were bought for **different reasons** and that consequently a **new segmentation criteria was required**.

SUVs—sports utility vehicles—combined the feature of both a city-sleek large car with its spacious interior and an off-road vehicle given its elevated

---

From the above two mistakes followed: (1) the belief that low price PC clones (Apple, Epson, etc.) did not matter and (2) no exclusive rights with PC suppliers such as Microsoft (Windows) and Intel (chips) were negotiated, leaving them free to supply to other brands.

That was deemed as non-relevant by IBM due to the belief that the power of its image would lead clients to accept markup prices and inducing IBM to develop internally chips and software (and not with Intel and Microsoft).

The fourth phase saw the further declining of IBM with *networked computer systems* dominating the industry: not only with PCs (as mainframes or minicomputers) but also with stations, interface cards, nodes, routers, and switches.

And the fifth phase came when under the leadership of *L. Gerstner IBM adapted* to such a reality and consequently recovered (as described before in Section 4.1.1).

seat position and four-wheel drive. And these were consequently bought for *lifestyle reasons, not income.*[69]

And in the case of *minivans,* the distinction between vehicles for professional and personal use did not hold true anymore, as they were bought both as "larger cabs" for passenger transportation and became also a popular choice for larger families since their flexible seating arrangements provided simultaneously a spacious interior for passengers and easy access to cargo through sliding rear doors.

That the distinction between vehicles for professional and personal use was *blurring* was further enhanced by *light trucks* acquired both for commercial purposes and individual or small families' transportation.

The above examples illustrate that **unexpected successes** require a review of the theory of business, regardless if they come from **competition** or the operations of **our own company**.

And the same applies to **unexpected failures**. Our missteps. These, however, must be looked at carefully, at an interval of every one or two years, after due diligence and perseverance demonstrating that they are not due to tactical (marketing, manufacturing, etc.) errors.

4.2. How to Review the Theory of Business

Figure 17 summarizes the reality hypothesis of the examples discussed in the previous section, and Figure 18 does the same for the cases used in Chapter 2, when the concept of theory of business was introduced:

---

[69]Lifestyle segmentation became since then increasingly used. Distinguishing among urbans, nomads, sportives, traditional, minimalists, and so on. It is found useful by an ever-wider range of industries, from restaurants to hotels and including garments, beverages, and food retail. Chrysler was first to use it with such a great success that General Motors followed immediately.

Reality assumptions / Examples	Type	Statistical trends/facts	Culture at large	Individual psychology	Technical	Institutional (administrative/legal)	Direct Competition? Exists?	Quality?
Change pace	Sears	Farmers — Number / Isolation	Specific needs				No	-
	IBM recovery in this millennium				Best common way to process information is through network computer systems		Yes	High
	Gorillas	People working from home	Percentage refraining from personal contacts	Lower importance attributed to selection of groceries than to fresh products		Legal shutdowns	Yes	Medium (1)
Unexpected successes	Competition — IBM versus Apple's PCs				PCs as strong alternatives to mini and mainframes		Yes	High
	Chrysler (minivans, SUVs)		Market segmentation based on multipurpose vehicles and lifestyle				Yes	High
	Ours — General Motors (light trucks)			Market segmentation based on multipurpose vehicles			Yes	Medium (2)

Figure 17 Reality assumptions of previous section examples

Notes:

(1)   There were other companies supplying fast home delivery but not so rapid (10 minutes) and including other products.

(2)   Medium and not high as competition, the companies did not fully understand clients' purpose when acquiring the vehicles with the consequence that its promotion was off target.

Nike, Dollar Shave Club, and SpaceX, regarding these companies at their inception.[70]

As Figures 17 and 18, although equivalent to, are a more detailed version of previous figures addressing the same examples, they indicate that **reality assumptions** can be of **six main types**:

1. *Statistical* trends;
2. *Culture* at large (regarding all or large parts of society);

---

[70]As companies grow they develop resources and, thus, they have the option to test their business theories more thinly.

Reality assumptions / Type / Example	Statistical trends/facts	Culture at large	Individual psychology	Technical	Institutional (administrative/legal)	Direct competition? Exists?	Quality?
Nike	Running is booming — On-track (competition), Off-track (joggers); Feasible to undercut competition prices with Japanese suppliers	Jogging acceptance by others	Individualism	Specialized sneakers matter for performance; Shoes should have five characteristics: Light, Comfortable, Minimizing injuries, Gripping power, Outstanding design	Anti-jogging laws	No	-
Dollar Shave Club	Blades prices are high (far lower profitable prices can be practiced)		In-store buying is a hassle; People resent both prices and the buying hassle	Blades are a commodity; Home delivery of blades is feasible		No	-
SpaceX	Three billion people of isolated or poor countries cannot afford Internet at present prices; In highly developed countries many companies will only pay cheaper prices for satellites information			Possible to be a low-cost satellite service provider (to be the Southwest Airlines of the space)		No	-

Figure 18 Reality assumptions of Chapter 2 examples

3. *Psychological* (at a more micro level than culture);
4. *Technical;*
5. *Institutional* (including administrative and legal); and
6. *Direct competition*: if it exists or not. And in the former case how strong it is. In the latter case, the business theory is then innovative, and all things equal, so much better.

It is useful to analyze how to test these **six** types of reality hypothesis, by first going over each one, column by column, and then, across all lines using the examples of Gorillas and Nike.[71]

The answer **to competition** (right-side column of Figures 17 and 18) is straightforward, keeping in mind that it can be direct, if it pertains to the same market segment, or indirect when belonging to other segments of the same industry.

Existing and new entrants are bad news for the company (although good for the consumer) and must be accounted for, both for benchmarking and for eventual changes in tactics: pricing, promotion, and so on. The answer to the question of competition facing each firm is given at the right-side column of Figures 17 and 18.

Two aspects are noteworthy here.

First, although the concern here is foremost with direct and not indirect competition; if not even the latter exists, so much better, and such a case should be noted in the table signifying that the company is creating a new industry. Nevertheless, the information of Figures 17 and 18 happens to refer always to direct competition only as there are always indirect competitors.

---

[71] This section's analysis is quite detailed and, thus, most useful for the specialized reader; for the general reader, it will be enough to skim Figures 21 and 22 and then go directly to Section 4 3 in Page 95.

Then besides the existence (or not) of direct competition, there is the question of how strong is it? What is its level? Is it fulfilling most clients' needs and so getting the job done or rather performing poorly? That is an important distinction to be also acknowledged in Figures 17 and 18.

In the former case, competitive advantage cannot come from the theory of business but only from the other three competitiveness drivers: business model, strategy, and/or tactics.

However, to make the theory of business explicit remains important to remind the company why it makes sense—what it is paid for and, thus, to be able to periodically check if it still remains true.

Then there is column of the **institutional aspects** (legal, administrative) exemplified in the case of Gorillas, with the imposed shutdowns in multiple countries, and in Nike with the progressive disappearance of anti-jogging laws in U.S. cities during the 1960s.

Technical assumptions refer to subjects such as: What is the best common way of information processing (e.g., IBM in this millennium in Figure 17)? How good are PCs as alternatives to mini and mainframes (IBM vs. Apple)? Do specialized sneakers improve performance (Nike in Figure 18)? Do they have the five characteristics of (1) lightness, (2) comfortable, (3) minimize injuries, and (4) have gripping power, as well as (5) an outstanding design to fit the individualistic personality of runners (to be addressed below)?

Such information is first to be given by technical experts and then its relevance judged by management, something one cannot do without, as the introduction of smartphones by Apple demonstrates.

In as early as 2006, **Nokia** possessed the technology. However, it failed to follow suit to Apple as its engineers believed that the iPhone was too expensive and had the serious technology flaw of working solely on second-generation networks. Thus, following the engineers advice, Nokia delayed market entry. Meanwhile, consumers queued during the night to buy iPhones.

Both culture at large and individual psychology are assumptions whose evaluation depends on soft data: How different are the needs of farmers compared to suburban and urban consumers (in the case of Sears)? How afraid are people that personal contacts will create the risk of getting COVID-19 (useful in the case of Gorillas)? How much of a hassle is it to buy in-store blades and to what extent people resented doing that, as well as the high prices maintained by Gillette, Schick, and others?

There are finally the assumptions whose information depends on **statistics**.

For instance, in the case of Sears, what is the number of farmers? And in order to evaluate their degree of isolation: What is the percentage of farmers owning a car? What percentage of farmers are serviced by frequent public transportation? Furthermore, what share of the U.S. geography is covered?

For Gorillas, what is the number of people working from home? For the Dollar Shave Club, how high are the prices of Gillette, Schick, Personna, and other brands of blades? And what are the lowest costs of imported blades (which Dollar Shave Club started buying from South Korea)?

In short: **hard data** provide the answer for (1) *statistical trends and facts*, (2) *technical assumptions*, (3) *institutional rules and laws*, and (4) *the type of existing competition*. And **soft data** inform on *cultural* and *psychological* *aspects*.

Having analyzed Figures 17 and 18 column by column, let us now focus on, for example, the two lines of **Gorillas** and **Nike** to see how they would go about reviewing their theories of business.

In the case of **Gorillas, four numbers** are important: (1) the number of people *working from home*, (2) the number of *shutdowns* and *how long* they were, (3) what percentage of the population refrains from *personal contacts*, and (4) the *importance* attributed by consumers to the purchase of groceries (rice, milk, pasta) versus that of fresh products (meat and fish), with the consequence of greater or smaller willingness of having the former home-delivered, without previous inspection.

And those same numbers are also relevant to evaluate demand and the level of markup prices and delivery fees consumers are willing to pay for having groceries home-delivered in 10 minutes.

Statistics provide information on the number of people working from home (Figure 19) and shutdowns (Figure 20), while *surveys* are necessary to know the extent to which persons refrain from personal contacts and, thus, the importance attributed to home delivery (83 percent of consumers believe the latter minimizes chronic diseases and over two-thirds— 68 percent—are willing to pay a premium for it).

From **Figure 19**, it can be concluded that after a peak in 2021, there was a decline in 2022 of the number of employees working from home—both in Europe and in the United States.

And **Figures 20-A and B** indicate that the number of shutdowns in the United States, Canada, UK, and European Union after having peaked in 2020 were null in 2022.

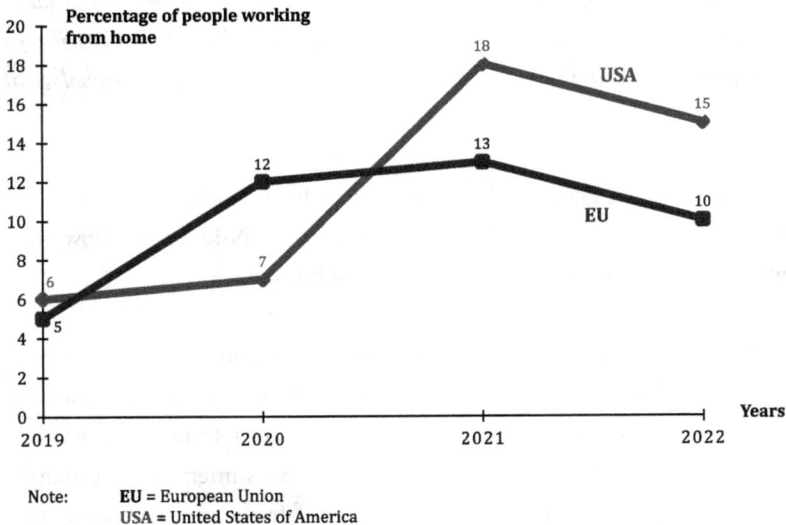

Note: EU = European Union
          USA = United States of America

Figure 19 Percentage of people working from home

Source: Eurostat and United States Census Bureau

Number of European Union countries with shutdowns

26   26

0   1 **Years**
2019   2020   2021   2022

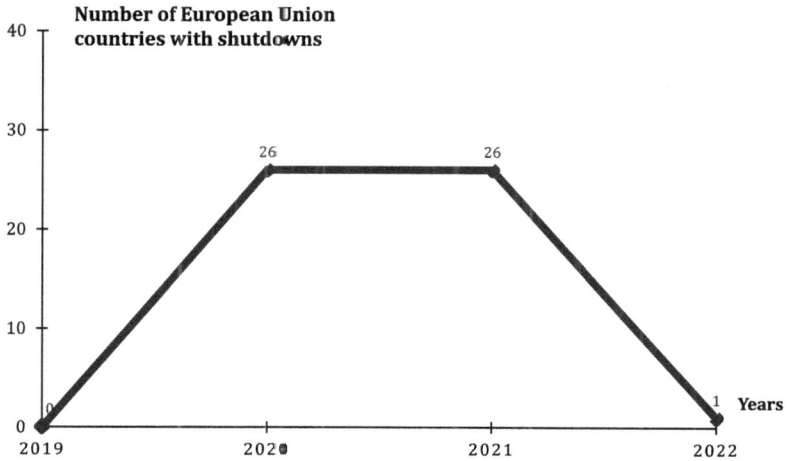

Figure 20-A Shutdowns

Source: Wikipedia

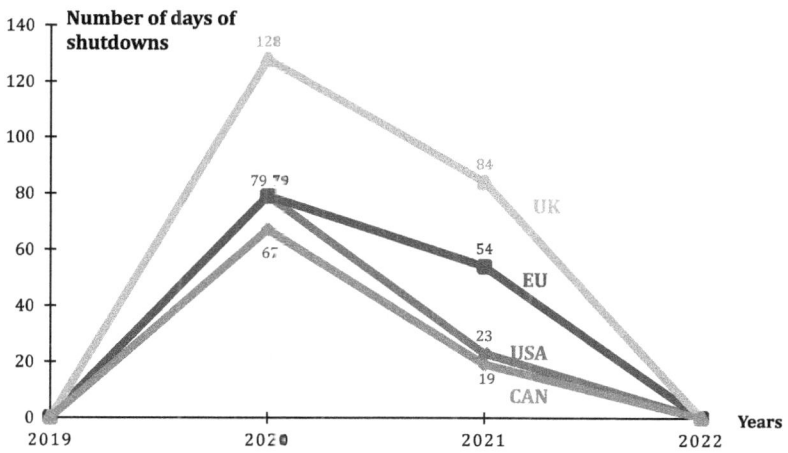

Number of days of shutdowns

128

79 79   84
                          UK
67   54
                    EU
              23   USA
              19   CAN

2019   2020   2021   2022 **Years**

Note: UK = United Kingdom
          EU = European Union
          USA = United States of America
          CAN = Canada

Figure 20-B Shutdowns

Source: Wikipedia; World Population Review

The above numbers explain why, being born in May 2020 and after raising $3 billion, Gorillas profits and cash losses forced it out of the market in December 2022 (just 2.5 years later), together with a long list of direct and indirect competitors from GoPuff to Fridge No More, to Buyk, Jokr, and so on, which have also disappeared.

The *only* companies that remained profitable in the food delivery business were those providing *high value*-added food, be they own prepared meals such as Gousto[72] or picking up from *restaurants* as in the case of Uber Eats or Instacart.

And from here, **three** inferences follow:

First, the *quick commerce business working from dark supermarkets* (own warehouses) was launched on a **temporary foundation,** and, consequently, the demand for this service was doused by the return to normal life.

Second, the decline was as sharp as the initial success, with less and less hunger for ultra-fast grocery delivery services.

And *finally*, only those companies that adapted to other type of deliveries (not merely quick groceries but higher value added) remain alive and thrive.

Let's now turn to **Nike** and analyze how would Phil Knight test the theory of business when he launched the venture (at later stages, the questions would be the same, but the numbers of the answers are different, naturally).

Nike was based on the following *reality assumptions*:

First, the number of people running *is booming*. Although only a few in 1964, the trend was exponential in terms of both on-track and off-track.

---

[72]A British meal kit retailer with 55 recipe options per week with box kits delivered to consumers doorsteps.

On the former and in the absence of better, direct, information, substitute **statistics** could be, for example (1) the number of running competitions per year in the United States, (2) the number of athletes participating in them, (3) how many athletes participated in the Boston Marathon (the most famous of all), (4) the number of marathons per year, or (5) how many marathon finishers there were (Figures 21–23).

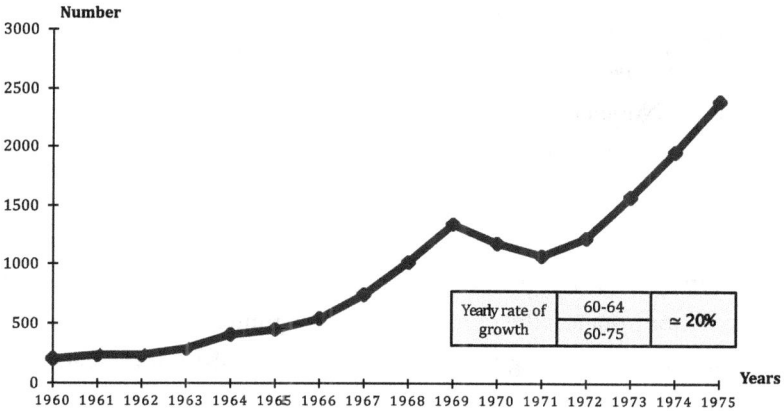

Figure 21 Number of runners in Boston Marathon

Source: Boston Marathon

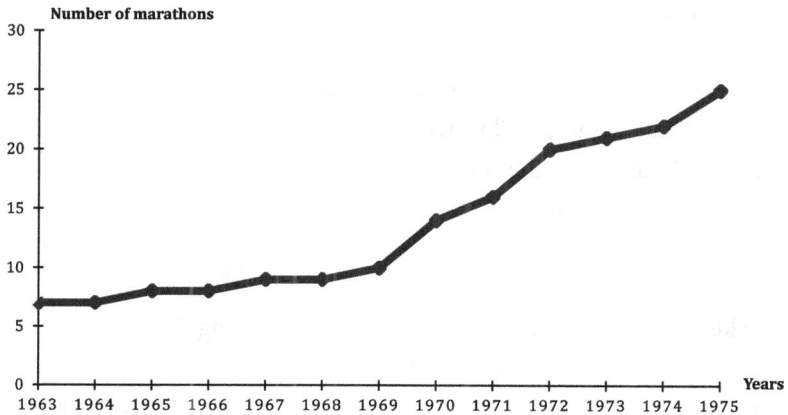

Figure 22 Number of marathons in United States

Source: Wikipedia

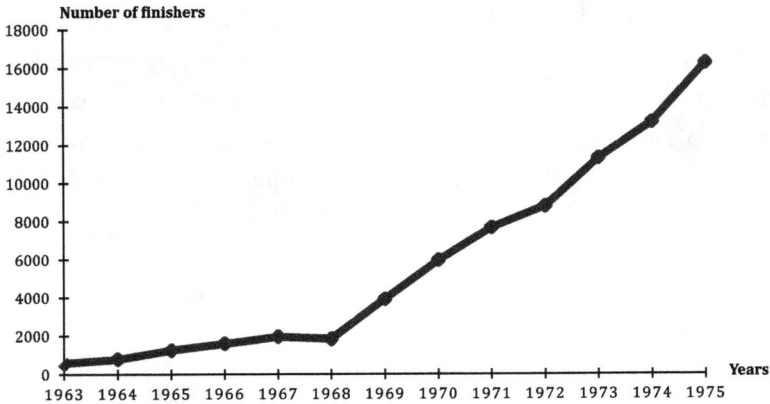

Figure 23 Number of finishers in marathons in United States

Source: Association of Road Racing Statisticians (ARRS)

And so the point here is **threefold**. There are *several* types of useful data; the greater the *variety*, the better; and from some statistics others can be deduced: for instance, the number of off-track runners (joggers) could be estimated by multiplying by a factor the number of Boston's marathon participants.

Best to determine that factor would be to start with Phil Knight's judgment, as he himself was a runner and immersed in the "tribe"; later, that could be replaced by market surveys; and, finally, time would bring statistics from third parties such as running associations.

Statistics are also the source to test another Nike's reality assumption, namely that it was possible with Japanese imports to undercut the prices maintained by the dominant players of Adidas, Puma, Reebok, and Converse: The first Nike's sneakers were sold at $6.95, far below competition.

Market surveys could also judge jogging receiving increasing social acceptance, together with **statistics** on the number of towns having anti-jogging laws (frequent in the 1960s), while **psychological tests** are the way to evaluate the degree of runners' individualism (important for the sneakers' outstanding design as discussed in Chapter 2).

The sneakers technical requirements of comfort (since the sneakers are used for long periods, and every time an exercise was practiced), minimizing injuries, and gripping could again be evaluated by **surveys**, and it is also feasible to evaluate the latter two aspects via **laboratorial tests**, and, in particular, to evaluate the lightness of Nike's shoes against the models of Adidas, Puma, Reebok, and other competitors.[73] [74]

Figure 24 summarizes this section indicating that some information is *hard* (*statistical*), other *judgmental*. Some statistics are *precisely those* needed (on-target), while others are *the closest possible substitutes.*

Whatever the case, they are nevertheless always useful as they contribute to clarify **how true** Nike's theory of business was at its inception with a

---

[73]As per Chapter 2, at the inception of Nike, technology was focused on producing ever-lighter shoes, as similar as possible to run with sockets or barefoot (provided the shoe gave enough protection for the feet).

Today, however, the search for *lightness* has been replaced by the *impulse* given by high soles made of various types of foams. The maximum allowed sole height in competition is 40 mm.

[74]**Six** aspects are here noteworthy. **First** and regarding the five characteristics (lightness, gripping, comfort, minimize injuries, and design) one must distinguish between importance for the buyer and how good each brand (Nike, Adidas, Puma) was on each of the characteristics.

Second, not all five characteristics have to have the same importance. It can vary.

Third, the importance of the criteria also varies from on-track (one segment) to another segment (off-track): for instance, design being far more important for joggers than professionals.

Fourth, even within each segment (e.g., on-track), their relevance was not the same among several niches: In short-distance races, comfort becomes less relevant than in longer-distance ones such as half or full marathons.

Fifth, it is possible to compute the *competitiveness of each brand*. If, for example, Nike in a scale of 1 to 7 receives 6 in all five criteria and the competition a 5 on average, the competitive advantage of Nike is 20 percent $= \dfrac{6-5=1}{5}$

Or if Nike has still in average a 6 but competition now a 4, then the competitive advantage is 50 percent $= \dfrac{6-4=2}{4}$; and so on.

Finally, a good book on this subject is *Jobs to Be Done* by Anthony W. Ulwick (2016).

Information — For	Phil Knight's evaluation	Statistics — Direct: Number competitions	Statistics — Number participants: Competitions	Statistics — Number participants: Boston marathon	Market surveys	City laws	Lab tests
Number runners — On-track (professional)	✓	✓	✓	✓	✓		
Number runners — Off-track (joggers)	✓	✓	✓	✓	✓		
Jogging is culturally accepted	✓				✓	✓	
Joggers are — Individualistic	✓				✓		
Joggers are — Wealthier	✓				✓		
Joggers are — Comfort	✓				✓		
Importance and advantage over competition of — Minimize injuries	✓				✓		✓
Importance and advantage over competition of — Grip	✓				✓		✓
Importance and advantage over competition of — Lightness	✓						✓
Importance and advantage over competition of — Design	✓				✓		

Figure 24 Sources of information to test Nike's theory of business

direct impact on (1) *market sales* and (2) on the *price* that can be charged for its product (Figure 24).

Then on its turn, market sales will be translated into company sales through market share. And the price to be charged depends on how much better relative to competition the product satisfies customer's needs (of lightness, gripping power, comfort, minimize injuries, and individualism) and the elasticity of demand (as per Point 5 of 74th footnote).

And in any case, the above information must be periodically checked to validate the theory of business and draw projections for sales. **But how often?**

4.3. When to Review the Business Theory

Let's use the two examples of *Gorillas* and *Nike* to answer that question since they are contrasting cases regarding the circumstances under which they were born.

Gorillas was launched in a crisis, a rupture of normal circumstances. *Nike* was based (to use Peter Drucker's expression) on the future that had already happened: that is, an upstart trend at which Phil Knight jumped very early on to stay ahead of the curve.

And so, different birth circumstances have distinct consequences in terms of when to review the business theory.

4.3.1. Gorillas: The Case of Firms Based on Ruptures

There are many opportunities due to **crisis.** For instance, the COVID-19 epidemic was the reason behind Fogblock, the anti-fog solution for glass-wearers when using a mask. And other opportunities followed: the boom on telemedicine, online education, fitness and wellness apps, sanitization services, and, of course, quick food delivery, in the case of Gorillas of groceries in 10 minutes.

As crisis come and go, numbers must be checked **quite frequently** so that alerts occur in due time: that reality assumptions are becoming obsolete, consequently threatening the business survival and requiring the company to change gears before it is too late. *Before a problem becomes an emergency.*

In the quick food delivery business that is illustrated by, for example, *Getir*, which (on top of quick groceries deliveries from own warehouses like Gorillas) started including deliveries from other stores to fill idle time of workers.

Or by *Instacart*, which relies on partnerships with existing groceries stores, acts as a personal shopper to fulfill and deliver consumer orders in a variety of stores such as pharmacies, office supply stores, and pet stores, and even uses its platform to offer retailers tools for warehouse fulfillment, ad support, and customer insights. As a consequence, Instacart has remained profitable even after the end of the COVID-19 crisis.

In short, companies born in crisis and because of crisis must have their theories of business reviewed very frequently say, every quarter. In the case of Gorillas, it would be the percentage of people working from home, the number of days of shutdowns, and so on.

But this high frequency is for the **exceptional case** of firms started during **disruptions**.

That is not the case of most businesses, such as *Nike*.

4.3.2. Nike: When to Review the Business Theories of Companies Based on Long-Term Trends

Nike was created on the assumption that there would be a high and consistent growth of the number of joggers, as well as participants in competitions such as marathons and on-track professional athletes.

In instances as that of Nike, the reasons for periodic checks are **twofold**: **change** and unexpected **successes**.

One must first of all avoid that a firm becomes a weathercock, a weather vane, constantly changing directions. The selected business model and tactical policies (marketing, operations, finance, human resources) *must be allowed time to work—to prove themselves.*

And so, only after considerable **perseverance** it makes sense to consider changing gears.

Also it is advantageous that the theory of business review becomes a **routine**, not something out of the normal, which urgent matters at hand to attend to will always postpone it, leading to constant procrastination.

Thus, in order to make periodic analysis of an established procedure, it is advisable to associate it with the budgeting and/or the strategic planning process: the series of meetings to systematically review the geographical areas, industries, and segments the company operates in. The former is done yearly. The second, strategic planning, sometimes also does so and other times it may do so every two years.

The **planning cycle** (in Figure 25) starts with reviewing the *theory of business*. Then comes the *strategy*. Next the *business model* (to be analyzed in the next chapter) and finally the *tactical plans*: of finance (budget), marketing, human resources, and so on (which is the subject of the last chapter).

4.4. Conclusion

This chapter analyzed the **why**, **how**, and **when** to review the business theory of a firm.

But the same questions apply to the business model, which is the focus of the next chapter.

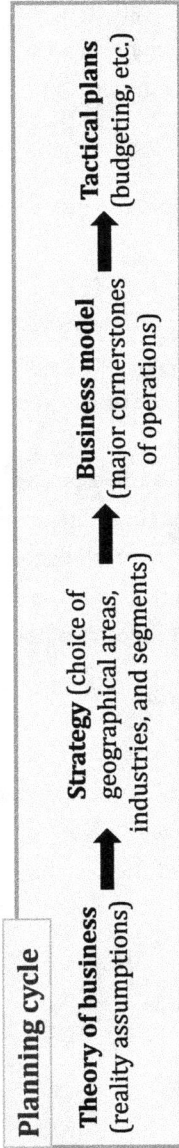

25A

Planning cycle

Theory of business (reality assumptions) → **Strategy** (choice of geographical areas, industries, and segments) → **Business model** (major cornerstones of operations) → **Tactical plans** (budgeting, etc.)

25B

Reasons to incorporate the review of the theory of business in the planning cycle / Consequences	Facts	Change and unexpected successes	Allow time for the business model tactics to work	Routine
Must be done		✓		
Not too frequently		✓	✓	
Associate with other plans reviews				✓

Figure 25 When and how to review the theory of business for companies based on long-term trends

CHAPTER 5

Why, When, and *How* to Review the Business Model

There is nothing constant except... change.
(Heraclitus, Greek philosopher, 535 BC—475 BC)

To change is to improve; to change often is perfection.
(Winston Churchill)

Let's briefly review the *why*, *when*, and *how* to **review the business model**.[75]

5.1. Why

The reason is **threefold**. *First*, we want to make *sure* there is *no better way*. *Second*, sometimes the business model *drifts away*, slowly, step by step, and unwantedly at times, creating after some time a *gap* between the initial/theoretical business model and the present/actual one.

In either of the above cases, an *opportunity cost* arises as performance is not optimized.

And then there is a *third* reason: In spite of strong theories of business, companies sometimes fail repeatedly to earn *profits*.

For some time, shareholders may accept that, due to expectations, incentivized by the originality of the business theory, and also because they have invested already some money in the business.

But after some time, they always throw their hands in the air and give up. Let's look at a few examples.

---

[75]A literature review on these three questions reveals that (1) the need to review is consensual, but information is lacking on (2) when and (3) how.

Indeed, many studies recognize that business models must be updated (e.g., Osterwalder et al., 2020; van der Pijl et al., 2020; Maucuer et al., 2019).

And several articles and books also stress that the business model scrutiny must be ever more frequent due to "uncertainty, fast change, technical disruptions, digital transformation and even environmental and social concerns" (e.g., Ademi et al., 2021; Vatankhah et al., 2023; Aagaard, 2024).

And finally, many other works exemplify the benefits of probing the business models, be it to multinationals (Essbaa et al., 2025), new technology companies (Löfsten et al., 2025) or small firms (de Villiers Scheepers et al., 2024). Whatever.

In short, the imperative for review is consensual. But the questions of when and how to go about it remain unanswered.

5.1.1. Is There a Better Way?

Shai Agassi and **Elon Musk** both created almost simultaneously their electric car companies—the former in Israel, and the latter in the United States. The first failed, and the second succeeded.

The theory of business was basically the same. Shai Agassi gave a presentation at the annual Davos meeting in Switzerland under the question of *what is the one thing I would do, to make the world a better place?* The answer: an *oil-free world.*

How? Through electric, not hybrid cars, since the latter are like mermaids: If one wants a woman one gets a fish and if one wants a fish one obtains a woman.

However, *Musk's* business model had **two major advantages** over *Agassi's,* which helped it avoid running out of cash: first, the car was **in-house built** (and not subcontracted to Renault Nissan, which ended up producing a non-cost competitive Sedan for Israel).[76]

And on top of that, Tesla benefited from several **financial policies** nonexistent in the case of Agassi's Better Place firm: prepaid orders of large quantities of vehicles, extensive government support both with direct financing and tax credits, and support from the financial markets through an IPO: initial public offering.

These **differences** explain why, in spite of delays in production and thus flirting with cash starvation and bankruptcy, Tesla in the end prevailed and Shai Agassi went under (in 2013).[77]

---

[76]The Tesla business model was characterized by: (1) high degree of vertical integration (with most parts done in-house) and (2) with the exception of the lithium batteries which were acquired.

[77]Together with two Agassi **strategic mistakes**: (1) wrong choice of model for Israel (a sedan instead of a subcompact) and (2) geographic dispersion, it added Israel to the Tokyo taxi market where it achieved considerable success.

SolarCity is another example of how a business model can make a great difference.

When it started, the industry was incipient, but the company came to be a major success based on **three main factors**: (1) *global service* with Solar-City both building and installing the panels and, thus, providing simplicity; (2) *lower panel prices* due to scale economies and in-house production; (3) *less risk to the clients*, as before the contract, SolarCity evaluated with a software whether there was enough sunlight to make the panels worthwhile, the panels were rented not bought, contracts could be passed on or canceled with the house sale, maintenance was part of the contract, and it included the option of changing for more efficient panels whenever they became available.

And then there were four **additional features**: the offer of solar roofs instead of ugly panels, the availability of storage batteries, the use in part of non-direct distribution through large operators such as Walmart and B2B on top of B2C marketing (Intel and other major corporations became clients).

Thus, to benchmark the initial design of the business model is always important. Isn't there a better way?

But then, there is another reason that makes testing it advantageous.

5.1.2. The Business Model Drifting Away

Sometimes, the basic pillars of operations are well set initially, but with time, little by little, small changes occur and, thus, the business model unwantedly drifts away and stops implementing the theory of business. Marks & Spencer illustrates that.

During the last half of the twentieth century, Marks & Spencer became the leading UK retailer with a business theory based on **three** assumptions:

1. There was no department store offering home goods, clothes, and food targeting the **middle and middle-upper** classes;

2. Contrary to other UK large department stores whose main competence was the ability to buy well (e.g., Woolworth, C&A)[78] or targeting the upper end (Harrods the ultrarich and Selfridges), Marks & Spencer's middle and middle-upper social classes were willing to pay higher prices as long as they obtained a **fair value for money** through a commitment for quality (good buys with high quality for the price level); and

3. It was the retailer, not the manufacturer, that for being in direct contact with the customers, **best knew their needs**.

In short, a department store focused on middle and middle-upper classes, for home goods, clothes, and food and pulling the consumers' needs to the manufacturers instead of pushing suppliers goods to the clients.

To implement such a theory of business, Marks & Spencer developed a **business model** based on:

a. Assuming **total initiative** and **control** for products *designing*, developing the *prototypes*, and finding the *best factories with*

b. A **decentralized** (to be as close as possible to the client) **decision-making process for orders** (of products, models, and quantities).

The result was that Marks & Spencer was the first UK retailer to achieve a billion pounds of profit (in 1998).

However, only six years later, in 2004, profits were down to 145 million pounds, and a new CEO (Stuart Rose) was hired to perform a turnaround.

Why?

Under the concern of being responsive to clients' needs, decisions on products and models were taken at ever-lower hierarchical levels by

---

[78]Marks & Spencer started as a penny bazaar for home goods. Its slogan was: Don't ask the price; it's a penny.

assistant buyers who lacked the required experience. In the words of the CEO Stuart Rose, "*by the spring of 2004 I immediately realized that the previous management's idea of delegating decision making to the lowest possible level had gone horribly wrong.*"[79]

With assistants deciding on orders of 30 and 40 million pounds without prior senior management signing-off, inventory without any upward commitment reached 300 million pounds and total inventory 3 billion pounds. Since year sales were 8 billion pounds that represented a 35-week inventory.

The resulting problems of such extensive delegation were **twofold**: (1) *lack of expertise* and (when stock piled up) and (2) the tendency of pushing (into the customer) the manufacturer's products instead of *pulling* these from the clients into factories.[80]

And so inventory, besides its *huge level*, had *two* other **flaws**:

- Many **core** products were both dowdy and high-priced with innumerous sub-brands without a following; and there were as well
- Many **noncore** products such as financial services, ultrahip furniture, and clothing for young trendy teenagers that the new CEO Stuart Rose decided immediately to part ways with.

Profits soon recovered (from 145 million in 2004 to 405 million in 2006 and then all the way up) through measures *such as* (1) re-centering the product line, (2) cutting on stock by increasing the hierarchical levels at which orders were made, (3) creating a top management job with the

---

[79]Back in fashion: How we're reviving a British icon; *Harvard Business Review*, May 2007.
[80]In his *HBR* article, Stuart Rose refers that frequently after assistants had triumphantly pointed out that a particular fabric had been made in a super fantastic factory…, they would confess that they had no idea whatsoever if such a product characteristic made any difference to the customer and thus if it had any impact on margin or volume.

exclusive role of controlling inventory (4) that reported directly to the CEO, (5) instituting weekly meetings with the CEO's presence, and (6) creating various supporting teams.

Other measures included, with the help of suppliers, reducing costs to the tune of 100 million pounds from the supply chain and restructuring logistics to decrease transportation costs, which enabled the company to reduce prices while maintaining quality.

The **main point** here is that Marks & Spencer had initially **both** *a sound theory of business and a good business model.*

However, slowly, with time, almost imperceptibly, due to ever-greater delegation, the business model **drifted away** and **stopped implementing** the business theory.

Thus, the aforesaid turn of events in the business—that is, the business model's drifting away—required a major reorganization and illustrated another reason why business models must be **periodically reviewed**: *They tend to drift away.*

5.1.3. Sales but No Profits

There is **a third** instance when a business model review is in order: *Company sales increase but fail to achieve profit level.*

In such cases, the market is signaling that there is a **need for the product**. But the way the firm operates **fails to transform** client satisfaction into value for the company—because of the business model.

Uber, Glovo, Bolt, and Gorillas exemplify that no company, regardless how innovative its business theory is, can go indefinitely without remunerating its shareholders.

Figure 26 compares the services offered by the above four companies at their start and at early 2024.

Companies / Services	Uber Initially	Uber 1/1/2024	Bolt Initially	Bolt 1/1/2024	Glovo Initially	Glovo 1/1/2024	Gorillas Initially	Gorillas 1/1/2024
Car rental	✓	✓		✓				
Car rental options (6 persons + luxury + wheelchair, etc.)		✓		✓				
Shared rides (pool)		✓						
E-scooters and bikes		✓		✓				
Restaurants deliveries		✓		✓	✓	✓		
Software taxis platform			✓	✓				
Software licensing				✓				
Local franchises				✓				
Supermarkets deliveries		✓				✓		
Non-food deliveries						✓		
Dark kitchens						✓		
Dark supermarkets				✓		✓	✓	✓

Figure 26 Comparison among Uber + Glovo + Bolt + Gorillas services

The firms *differ* in how they entered the market, the businesses that they added, and, thus, how they evolved into their present offering.

But they all *share* **one** characteristic (with the exception of Uber in 2018 and 2023—Figure 27-A): *None has ever been profitable.*

Gorillas was analyzed in the Chapter 4 and it was sold to Getir in December 2022.

Also, **Glovo,** which started in 2015 (Figure 27-C), not only had losses but increasingly so. As a result, it was sold in July 2022 to Delivery Hero.

And **Bolt** has also been losing money, year after year, raising the question of how long will it be able to stay in the market as an independent company (Figure 27-B).

The exceptions are **Uber** profits in 2018 and in 2023 of nearly $1 billion and $2 billion, respectively, but that represents only 8 percent of the sum of total losses in 10 years.

Year [1]	Profits/Losses (in billion dollars)-overall
2014	-0.7
2015	-1.6
2016	-3.6
2017	-4
2018	+0.997
2019	-8.506
2020	-6.768
2021	-0.496
2022	-9.141
2023	+1.887

[1] No information available for the years between 2009 and 2013.

Figure 27-A UBER (started in 2009)

Source: Uber annual reports; Business of Apps

Year	Profits/Losses (in million euros)-overall
2013	- 0,000957 (= -957 euros)
2014	- 0.395
2015	- 0.548
2016	- 0.361
2017	- 11.415
2018	- 60.583
2019	- 85.486
2020	- 44.918
2021	- 547.230
2022	- 72.197
2023	- 91.897

Figure 27-B BOLT (started in 2013)

Source: Bolt annual reports

Year[1]	Profits/Losses (in million euros) - overall
2018	- 90
2019	- 238.5
2020	- 51.4
2021	- 474.8

[1] Only years there is data available for.

Figure 27-C GLOVO (started in 2015)

Source: Deal Room; The WageIndicator Foundation; Time news

Thus again the question: Is Uber at a turning point, or will it share the fate of Gorillas and Glovo and most likely that of Bolt as well?

5.2. When to Review

As with the theory of business (Section 4.3) the assessment must be:

- **Not too** frequent, and
- **Periodic**.

Not too frequent since to reevaluate the business model is—as the next section will discuss—hard work which requires much of top management time.

Thus, it is better for a company to avoid being a weathercock, too reactive to environmental changes without allowing the required time for tactical policies to produce results in operations, marketing, whatsoever.[81]

So a periodicity of **one year**, at most every **two years**, seems a good **trade-off** between the needs of frequency and the cost of investing the required time of doing it well.

And just as with the theory of business, time comes minimized if the business model review is done **together** with the budgeting process, or strategic planning cycle (choice of geographical areas, industries, and segments).

5.3. How to Review the Business Model

It is useful here to distinguish between **two** situations—companies working in *partnership*, such as a joint venture or with franchisees, and *stand-alone firms*.

5.3.1. Companies Operating in Alliance

When a firm is part of a network that encompasses a group of other reasonably autonomous entities, the first step in reviewing the business model is to consider *restructuring the terms of the alliance*.

And preferably to do that in such a way that it becomes a positive (not a zero) sum game where *all* parties benefit. Be it from greater control, standardization, centralization (and thus cheaper purchases), whatever.

McDonald's is an example.

---

[81]And so better not to follow some literature suggestions to review the business model when there are many *non-clients* (be they clients of other brands or non-category users), *new technology appears*, a disruption by *low market end* competitors occurs or there is a surge of *new competitors* of any kind.

At a very early stage, there was the S. Bernardino restaurant run by the McDonald brothers and Ray Kroc who had an agreement with them under which he:

- Had the right to open and franchise restaurants;
- Always cloning the products and speed system of S. Bernardino's;
- Any deviation had to be previously approved by the McDonald brothers (what never happened); and
- Kroc would receive a $950 franchise fee;
- Plus 1.9 percent of each restaurant's revenue, of which he would remit 0.5 percent to the brothers.

In short, periodic revenues were 1.4 percent (1.9 to 0.5 percent) on a (then) 15¢ hamburger.

And from such an agreement, two problems emerged: not enough profits and insufficient control.

Indeed, many outlets would decide on their own to add new products; change the content of hamburgers, fries, and milkshakes (the only three products); and modify how they were produced—the operations.

That made the situation **unsustainable** and proved a direct way into **bankruptcy** until the financial consultant **Harry Sonneborn** came along and told R. Kroc that he had got his business model wrong: He had to add an **additional item** to the agreement with the franchisees that would increase both the revenue and control.[82]

---

[82]The movie The Founder presents a dramatic (though apocryphal) scene when Harry Sonneborn, a financial consultant, overhearing Ray Kroc's plea for a loan in a bank, catches up with him in the street, and states the obvious: "Mr. Kroc I have been to your restaurants. They are great and full of clients. Thus sales must be booming. So, if you are not making a great deal of money there must be something very flawed with your business model: will you allow me to take a look at it?"

Kroc acquiesced, he reviewed McDonald's business model, suggested the change regarding the land and thus followed the world's largest franchise.

The item was the **control** of the **land**, which had the advantages of (1) augmenting R. Kroc's *income* without affecting seriously the profitability of the franchisees, (2) enforcing *standardization*, (3) attracting franchisees that although lacked cash had the required *entrepreneurial spirit*, and (4) providing bank guarantees to *expand the business*.

The above assessment required R. Kroc to negotiate with landowners a lease (which would include the building they would by themselves construct) and then pass the lease into the franchisees at a markup[83] or, alternatively, to get bank financing for the land, own it, and then again lease it out to the franchisees.[84]

The McDonald's brothers could not oppose R. Kroc's ownership of the land in the agreement with franchisees, since the contract with the brothers covered what happened *within* each restaurant and not how the business was structured.

To deal with the real estate, a separate company called Franchise Realty Corporation was created. A steadily larger income would flow as well as greater control of the quality of the franchisees by being their landlord, together with the ability of selecting franchisees by their entrepreneurial spirit, not their wealth.

Finally, the land enabled Kroc to fuel growth because it grew revenue per fixed costs, overcoming tiny operating margins and providing a guarantee for banks to finance the expansion of operations: Kroc had its first franchisee (in Illinois) in 1955. In 1956, there were already 19 stores. In 1957, their number was 40, and then 79 (in 1958), 145 (in 1959), 228 (in 1960), and so on.

With an additional source of income, R. Kroc became a very rich man. And with stronger standardization, franchisees benefited as well: no surprises for clients, quantity discounts from centralized purchases, better brand image, and management improvements to be shared among all through common experience.

---

[83]Kroc's markup over the lease cost started at 20 percent and later increased to 40 percent.

[84]If a franchisee owned the land already, Kroc would make him lease it to him and he would sublease it back.

Today, over 90 percent of McDonald's restaurants are franchise operations, and all franchisees pay rent to McDonald's with a monthly fee, or percent of revenue of sales.

McDonald's is worth $215 billion and the brand is worth around $190 billion, making it the fifth most valuable in the world after Apple, Google, Microsoft, and Amazon and ahead of Visa, Louis Vuitton, Master-Card, and Coca-Cola.

And it is the largest franchise in the world with more than 40,000 outlets operating in more than 100 countries and serving more than 70 million clients.

5.3.2. Stand Alone Companies

In this instance, **five** steps are involved in reviewing the business model (Figure 28).

First, what are the *major building blocks* of operations?

Second, how do they *relate/interact*?

Third (and regarding the above two), what are the *major differences* compared to *best-performing*:

3.1. Direct competitors; and

3.2. Indirect competitors, using same or similar technology.

Fourth, what are the *major alternatives* to do away with those differences?

Fifth, select the *best way(s)* based on:

5.1. Market impact, and

5.2. Technology feasibility.

Spotify, the leading music streaming company, is an illustration.

Its business model was analyzed at some length in Section 3.2 to illustrate how a wrong business model prevented performance and the required

Type of operations	Source			
A **In alliance** (network of companies)	**Restructure the partnership**	Creating *a positive sum game*		
		or		
		Obtaining *greater share* of the supply chain value		
B **Stand alone firm**	**Step**	**Content**		
	First	What are the *major building blocks?*		
	Second	How do they interrelate?		
	Third	*Major differences of the above regarding best performing competition*	3.1. *Direct*	
			+	
			3.2. *Indirect with same or similar technology*	
	Fourth	*Alternative types of actions* to remove the above differences		
	Fifth	Select *best* in terms of	5.1. *Market Impact*	
			+	
			5.2. *Technology feasibility*	

Figure 28 How to review the business model

changes performed on it. We will now use again Spotify's example to systematize the **steps** to follow when **reviewing** a business model.[85]

---

[85]A summary of Section 3.2 is as follows:

The music industry experienced **two** major changes in recent years.

First *streaming* replaced other forms (CDs, DVDs) as the greatest source of revenue. And **then** pirate sites as Pirate Bay, became increasingly substituted by *for profit firms* such as Apple Music, Amazon Music, YouTube Music, Tidal, Napster, and Spotify.

The latter dominates the market with a revenue of $16 billion in 2024 ($10.5 billion estimated for Apple Music, the largest competitor), a 32 percent market share (2.5–3 times that of each main competitor—Apple Music, Amazon Music, and YouTube Music) and consequently having a market value of $90 billion in 2024, quite above any other firm such as Tidal ($600 million worth).

So, both the proliferation of companies and the profitability of Apple Music (Apple Services which include Apple Music has positive gross and operating margins) demonstrates **the validity of the theory of business**, based on **three** tenets:

1. *Many people* enjoy listening to music: 93 percent of Americans do an average of 20 hours per week;
2. They prefer to do it with *streaming* (4 in 5 people); and
3. They are willing to leave pirates sites and *pay*. Although 30 percent of music streamers still use illegal methods, the number of subscribers has increased 10 times since 2015, numbering 700 million in 2023 and thus the global music streaming annual revenue augmented from $1 billion in 2012 to over $19 billion in 2023.

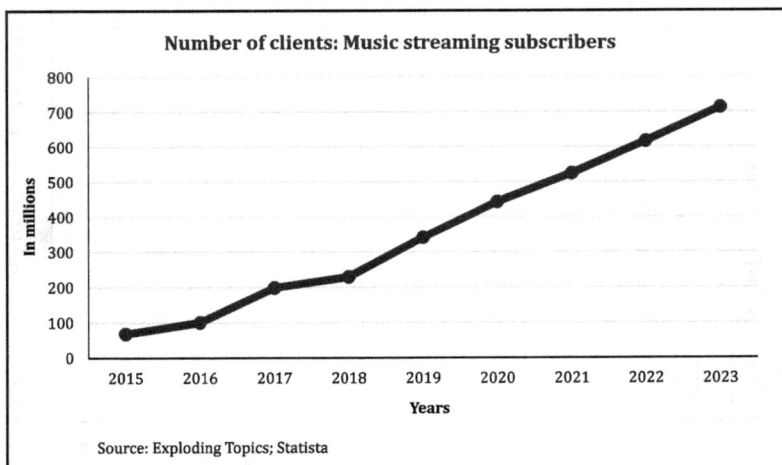

Number of clients: Music streaming subscribers

Source: Exploding Topics; Statista

However **in spite of** (1) having the *largest market share* (32 percent) and (2) *a sound theory of business* (the market is booming), Spotify *lost money for near two decades,* year after year, and increasingly so: Losses in 2022 were 430 million euros, and in 2023 reached 532 million euros. Finally in 2024, there was a profit of over 1.1 billion euros.

Since the upstart, Spotify's business model was characterized by the *absence of a platform* and the *offer of two options to subscribers: free* (no fees but with ads) and *premium* (pay but without ads)—Figure 29.[86]

MUSIC STREAMING COMPANIES			
Company	Platform (for other purchases)	Free (but with ads) option	Pay option
Spotify	No	Yes	Yes
Apple Music	Yes	No	Yes
Amazon Music	Yes	Yes	Yes
YouTube Music	Yes	Yes	Yes
Napster	No	No	Yes
Tidal	No	No	Yes

Figure 29 The basic pillars of the business model of music streaming companies

That left **Spotify** as the **sole** company, which *without a platform offered both a free and a pay option* as per Figure 29.

Indeed, some firms (Apple, Amazon, YouTube) benefited from already *existing platforms* created for other purposes (movies, books) while others did not (Napster, Tidal, and Spotify).

And some other companies offer subscribers **two options**: a *free* one (without fees but with ads and other limitations) and a *pay option* (under different plans): that is the case of Spotify, Amazon, and YouTube.

Still other organizations have only a pay option: Apple, Napster, and Tidal.

But offering (1) both a free and pay option and (2) without a platform, **Spotify** is the **only** one to do so.

---

[86]In June 2024, a third (basic) option was introduced, representing an in-between, the free and premium (pay) ones.

In the absence of a platform, the free-option role is to attract clients to the pay option. That is:

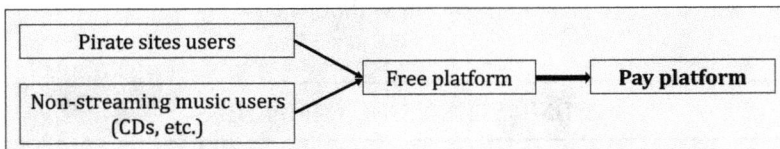

Let us now focus on the **two best, direct and indirect competitors** (Step 3 in Figure 28-B).

Apple Music[87] is the former since it has—after Spotify—the second largest market share and being profitable achieved in 2023 a gross margin of 2.6 times that of Spotify (71 percent against 27 percent).

And one of the best-performing indirect competitors is Canva,[88] an online graphic design site, consistently profitable since 2017 and a valuation that in the last years has oscillated between $30 billion and $40 billion.

Canva also like Spotify does not have an already existing platform created for **other purposes** and offers the two options of free and pay, but while a minority of Spotify users opt to pay, in the case of Canva 67 percent opt for paying.

In short, Spotify when compared to Apple Music (the best direct competitor) differs in that instead of a platform it offers a free option, and, with regard to Canva, it has exactly the same two options of free and pay, but in Canva these two differ more in terms of added value. That explains that almost two-thirds of users opt for pay (with one-third using it free), and in Spotify the percentages are nearly reversed (Figure 30).

---

[87] As there is no individual data for Apple Music, the best proxy is to refer to Apple Services which, besides Apple Music, includes iCloud, App Store, Apple TV, the gaming Apple Arcade, and others such as Apple Fitness and Apple Pay.
[88] Although not primarily a streaming company, Canva's platform, in order to allow users to create visual content such as presentations, posters, and documents, has incorporated into it some streaming-related features and technologies.

Type of competitors / Characteristics	Direct (Apple Music)	Indirect (Canva)
Already existing platform created for other purposes	Yes	No
Free option	No	Yes
Difference between free and pay options	-	Greater

Figure 30 *Differences of Spotify business model compared to two high-performing competitors*

From Figures 31 and 32, which show the difference between the benefits of free and premium plans in Spotify and Canva, one concludes that the most prominent **differentiating features are lacking in Spotify**:

- *For paying users*: Interaction, in terms of
  - Feedback (reports);
  - Suggestions (insights for teams and others);
  - Options to collaborate; and
- *For free users*: FOMO (fear of missing out); whenever using Canva, a free-option consumer is constantly reminded of what he or she is missing for not subscribing the premium plan: The user always sees paid and free templates on the same page (paid templates have a special icon) and sometimes also saving functions for editing templates that in the free plan are not available.

So in the case of Canva, besides other valences (e.g., 1 TB cloud storage for paying subscribers), personalization, and FOMO, create a greater difference between the free and paying plans. Thus, Canva has been constantly profitable in the last six years and Spotify never since the start until 2024, taking almost two decades to reach profitability. Only 40 percent in Spotify pay against 67 percent doing it in Canva and that in spite of Canva's fees being between 25 and 50 percent above Spotfy's (depending on whether the paying plan is individual or package/groups).

Characteristics	Free	Premium
Ads	Yes (between songs)	No
Sound quality	Worse	Better
Off-line downloads	No	Yes
Compatible with other devices (smart TVs, etc.)	No	Yes
Songs list	Smaller	Larger
Other features (create playlists, etc.)	No	Yes

Figure 31 Spotify has two types of clients

Characteristics	Free	Paid
Ads	No	No
Free users have a clear idea of what they are missing for not being paid	Yes	-
Cloud storage (1 TB)	No (only 5 GB)	Yes
Content	Worse	Better
Option to collaborate	No	Yes
Support priority	No	Yes (24 hours)

Users = 135 million	Two-third paid
	one-third free
Unicorn = 40 billion	
Profitable	

Figure 32 Canva has two types of clients

After defining the stepping stones of Spotify's business model and how they are different from best competitors, the **next step** is to ponder **changing them**, and we thus enter in Phase 4 of reviewing the business model in Figure 28-B of Page 113.

In the case of Spotify, that would mean *one of two things*: *abandoning the free option*, which, in the absence of a platform, would make it much harder to attract subscribers, as exemplified by Tidal and Napster whose value is 50 times lower than Spotify's.

The second option is to *join existing platforms* such as Facebook (now Meta Platforms Inc.), Microsoft, Twitter (now X), Tencent, ByteDance, or Alibaba.

Still a third possibility is to maintain the existing pillars of the business model (the free and premium options), but to change *their interaction*: to increase the number of clients who opt for paying. These as said earlier are at present a minority.

In other words, the *absence of a platform* increases the *difficulty of attracting* clients. And the *existence of a free option* makes it harder to augment the number of Spotify subscribers that *pay*.

Thus, it seems that the *advantages of premium (paying)* option *over the free option* are not large enough, creating a **structural flaw** in the business model.

And the increase in added value from the free to the premium option, can be done in **two** ways: *diminishing the free features*[89] or *augmenting the paid ones*.

---

[89]Examples are limiting the number of hours per day free subscribers can listen to music, taking out the possibility of creating playlists, shortening the song list, and so on. The question is: Will subscribers opt out from the free option or will they go to the premium one or even to... Pirate Bay?

As the former has the disadvantage of effacing its attraction power, it seems more sensible to focus on improving what is offered to paying customers.

Thus the best venues to improve the business model seem **twofold**.

First, to join a *platform*. And **second**, *increase the value added* of the pay option.

And **both** were done by Spotify. On the former, it has consistently enlarged its presence in **Apple's** iOS (iPhone operating system), including through legal battles as illustrated by the recent 2024 victory in European courts with an antitrust ruling that fined Apple with $2 billion.

And the second course of action was improving the value added of the pay option by, for example, introducing karaoke (in 6/2022), audiobooks (9/2022), or video music (3/2024)—Figure 33.

Building blocks	Adopted	Instead of
Platform	Increasing presence in Apple iOS	No action (as Canva)
Free option	Maintained	Discontinuing
		Decreasing its attractiveness
Pay option	Increase in value offered	Maintaining present services level

Figure 33 Spotify's decisions on business model changes

That is **how** the business model changes were implemented.

But the **how** (and as per the initial Figure 1 of the book in Page 3) pertains to tactics. And that is the subject of Chapter 6.

5.4. Conclusion

This chapter analyzed the **why, when,** and **how** to review the business model.

On the latter, there are **two** instances: when a company works in *partnership* (e.g., McDonald's) and when *it stands alone* (e.g., Spotify).

The aim of *restructuring a partnership* is (1) to obtain for the firm a greater share of the total value and (2) if possible creating a positive sum game.

For *independent companies*, there are five sequential steps: (1) *identifying the pillars*, (2) evaluating how they are *interrelated*, (3) *benchmarking against best competition* (both direct and indirect), (4) list of *alternative courses of action*, and (5) *select the best* in terms of market impact and technology feasibility.

But what about **implementing** the business model changes together with **improving** the way each pillar works? To boost each one's functioning? In terms of costs and value offered to subscribers?

Even when there are no business model modifications, it is important that they be periodically reviewed, as there are always parts of operations to improve.

These issues must be periodically addressed. And since they belong to **how** each pillar operates, to its specific valences, they fall into the realm of **tactics**: the subject (together with strategy) of the next concluding chapter.

CHAPTER 6

Conclusion: The Four Drivers (*Business Theory* + *Business Model* + *Strategy* + *Tactics*) as Prerequisites for Competitiveness

Experience without theory is blind.
(Immanuel Kant, eighteenth-century philosopher)

6.1. The Four Requirements for Profitability

The generality of business administration books refer to (sound) **strategy** and **tactics** as the requirements for performance.

However, as this book's examples have demonstrated, there are two additional necessary components: a good **theory of business** and a valid **business model** (Table 5).

And so, this chapter will perform two tasks before concluding.

First, stress again the importance of **all** four concepts using **Farfetch** as an illustration.

And then, given that this book focused extensively on the theory of business and the business model, **stress a few important elements regarding strategy and tactics**.

Table 5 The four components of business performance

Design	Implementation
Theory of business	Strategy
Business model	Tactics

6.2. The Example of the Unicorn Farfetch

Farfetch is a good example of how a company's fate depends on all four areas of (1) *the theory of business*, (2) *strategy*, (3) *the business model*, and (4) (its execution with) *tactics*.

Founded in 2008, the firm's aim was to become the Amazon for fashion luxury products working as a digital platform both for small independent boutiques and luxury brands with worldwide visibility, such as Gucci, Dior, and Yves St. Laurent.

And **business boomed**: *in sales, partners* (Farfetch came to have in its site goods of more than 1,400 individual boutiques), *countries* to which products were sold (above 190), and *international prizes* (nearly 20). The company went public in the New York Stock Exchange valued at $20 billion.

However, *profits failed to materialize.* And *repeatedly* so: except during two years (2021 and 2022 and 13 years after its launching), Farfetch always reported losses (to which it returned in 2023). Thus, in 2023 and after several downsizings, the risk of default forced Farfetch to accept being acquired by Coupang[90] and disappear from the market as an independent company. The CEO and founder left.

Why?

All **four** pillars required for business performance (Table 5) were causes.

Farfetch's **theory of business** at the upstart (2008) was that:

1. Demand for luxury products was *growing*;
2. *Online* shopping was growing too;
3. Many luxury individual boutiques had *no* adequate sites;
4. The same happened with *high-visibility* brands such as Versace or Louis Vuitton;
5. Consequently, there was a demand for a *site* with great diversity of luxury goods;
6. Most specially, if the site offered systematic *discounts.*

This theory had some **flaws**—some from the upstart, and others soon followed.

First, there were **demand problems**, since many shoppers prefer to buy luxury in person due to their characteristics and price (as of May 2021, the average price for clothing was $653; for shoes, $521; and for accessories, $633). That affected Assumption *Number 5* above.

---

[90]Coupang supplied a loan of $500 million to be paid with Farfetch capital.

Then there was a problem of **supply**, of securing product. Farfetch site made far more sense for individual boutiques that needed exposure than to high-visibility brands like Dior, Chanel, and Louis Vuitton, which shied away from being part of a large site with great diversity (incompatible with an image of exclusivity) that offered discounts and also offered pre-owned items.

Thus, over time, these and other world major brands developed their own digital platforms, which enabled higher control. And that went against Assumption *Number 4* above.

Those were the problems with the theory of business.

But then, given the difficulty of securing product, Farfetch's **strategy** changed from luxury fashion into *beauty* with the acquisition of Violet Grey, into *streetwear*. And also into *servicing* department stores (e.g., Harrod's) sites. And in these new areas competition was far stronger.

Then also the **business model** started drifting away as it came to include *second-hand items* and *vertical integration* with acquisitions that had to be managed and financed (NGG, Browns).

Finally, several major **tactical** mistakes were added, among them too many *headcounts*, accessories *prices* off the charts, and very thin *margins* (generally 30 percent).

In short, an (increasingly) faulty *theory of business. Strategic mistakes* (entry into new highly competitive segments). A *drifting business model* that not only failed to solve the above problems but also aggravated them. And *tactical flaws* including a staff that ballooned to more than 6,000.

And so **there were four factors at play in Farfetch's demise** illustrating that for an organization *optimization* all four are *necessary* conditions. And that for *survival* every single one of them is a very important *facilitator*. They must be done at least reasonably well.

This book did however concentrate, using several examples, on the importance of the *business theory* and the *business model*. It focused only on these two.

Examples on the former: Nike, Dollar Shave Club, Sears Roebuck, ATT, Chrysler, General Motors, SpaceX, Gorillas, among others.

On the latter, examples included SolarCity, Tesla, McDonald's, Marks & Spencer, and Spotify.

It may thus be useful now, and before summing up, to focus on how the other two, **strategy**[91] and **tactics**, differ and interact as per Figure 34 (initially presented in the Introduction).

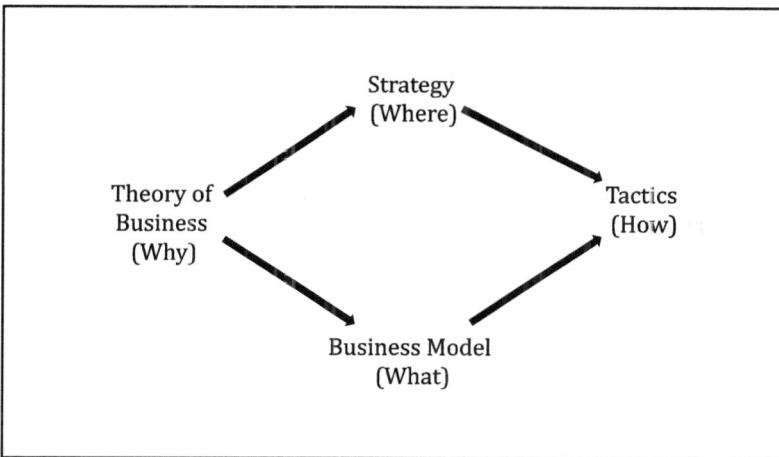

Figure 34 The four competitiveness drivers

---

[91]A *literature review* on the relationship between a business model and strategy and tactics can be *summarized* by:

First: "a business model is not the same as strategy but it has an important role in strategy implementation" (tactics) (Peric et al., 2017);

Second: "it remains difficult to distinguish a business model from conventional strategy" (Bigelow et al., 2021);

Third: "there is no well-defined view on the relation between a business model and strategy" (Ademi et al., 2021).

And so the above are this chapter's tasks.

6.3. Strategy and Tactics

The concept of **strategy** comes from warfare (Marshal Joffre) and respects **where** to fight, while *tactics* regards *how* to fight (Figure 35).[92]

Sometimes strategy is used with other meanings, but they all share two disadvantages, the first of which is that they are all **less useful.**

Indeed, sometimes strategy means the **important** (and tactics, the secondary, the less important).

However, since resources (time, energy, and money) are scarce, they should be dedicated only to the important. Thus, first things first, and, second things never (Peter Drucker).

And so all actions would be strategic, but none tactical. Strategy would be all and everything and a useless concept as it would not separate or draw a line between different aspects of reality.

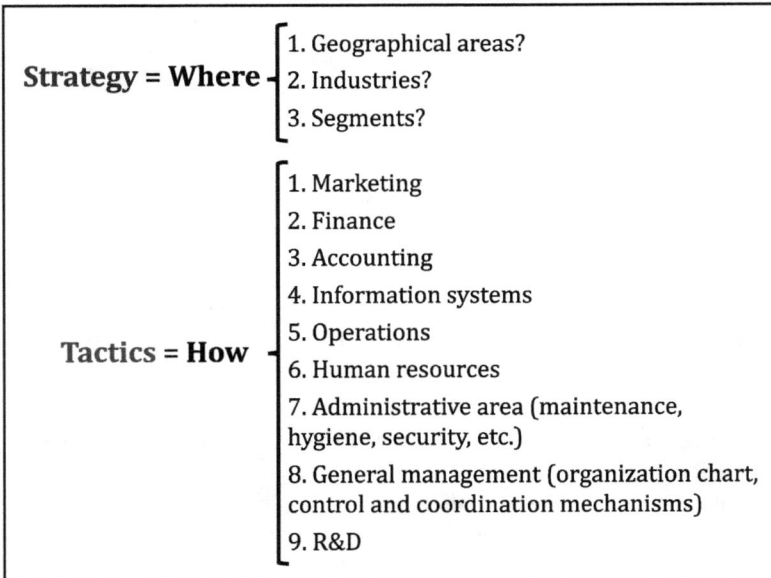

Strategy = Where
- 1. Geographical areas?
- 2. Industries?
- 3. Segments?

Tactics = How
- 1. Marketing
- 2. Finance
- 3. Accounting
- 4. Information systems
- 5. Operations
- 6. Human resources
- 7. Administrative area (maintenance, hygiene, security, etc.)
- 8. General management (organization chart, control and coordination mechanisms)
- 9. R&D

Figure 35 The difference between strategy and tactics

---

[92]On that see, for example, Sá (1999); or Sá (2005).

Other times by strategy is meant the **ends,** and, by tactics, the means.

But actions in organizations are nothing but a sequence of causes and consequences. For instance, when one hires an employee whose first task is to draw a list of advertising firms, to select the best, to conduct a promotion campaign, to increase sales, and to augment profits.

Except for profits (the ultimate end), and the initial task of hiring the employee (the initial cause), everything in the chain is simultaneously a means (to a subsequent end) and also, at the same time, an end (from the previous action). Thus, everything is simultaneously strategic and tactical, and both terms lose any meaning. And again one cannot separate strategy from tactics.

Still in other instances strategy is used to signify the **long term**, and tactics refers to the short term. But what is long term? Two years? One year? Why? And what if the year is a leap year? All the above is arbitrary. And therefore difficult to agree with the reason underneath (?) and, thus, recognize the utility.

Fortunately, there is a far better definition of strategy: **where** to compete (in terms of geographical areas, industries, and segments/niches). Then one clearly separates these types of business decisions from *tactics* (*how* to compete): how to advertise (marketing), how to issue bonds (finance), how to motivate (human resources), and so on (Figure 35).

The second advantage of using strategy as synonym to "where" is that when the word is used one knows **immediately** what is meant by it: one word, one concept. And so one does not have to ask: Do you mean strategy in the military sense (of where) or business sense (of whatever)?

One word, one meaning. And, therefore, **clarity**. On top of the advantage of separating in a nonambiguous way two types of decisions: the *where* from the *how*.

So, in business, if strategy means where, that refers to the choice of the (1) *geographical areas* (within them), (2) of *industries*, and (within them) (3) *segments/niches*. That is, where to compete. Where are the clients.

And although strategy follows from, and thus must be **compatible** with a theory of business, it is **not absolutely predetermined by it:** degrees of choice, of freedom, always remain.

Of the *three* elements of strategy (geography, industries, and segments), the theory of business *always* determines the industry and *sometimes* also the segment, *leaving open* the choice of the *geographic area*. The examples of **Nike** and **Getir** next will illustrate that.

Other times, the theory of business determines *only the industry* but *not the segments* (and neither the *geography*). And **Better Place** and **Tesla** will illustrate that.

Starting with **Nike** (and as we discussed in Chapter 2), its theory of business had five assumptions:

1. Racing (both off-track—joggers—and on-track—competition) was about to **boom**;
2. Racing required **specialized** shoes;
3. There were **no good-enough** specialized shoes;
4. Specialized shoes should have **five characteristics**:
   4.1. As light as possi-ble;
   4.2. Comfortable;
   4.3. Minimizing injuries;
   4.4. With gripping power;
   4.5. An appealing design; and
5. Japanese imports would allow to **undercut prices** of the dominant players in the industry: Adidas, Puma, Reebok, and Converse.

From Nike's business theory followed the definition of (1) **industry** (footwear), (2) **segment** (sports shoes), and even (3) **niche** within the segment (racing/running).

But there was no implication whatsoever regarding the **geographical area**. As it happened, Phil Knight's choice was first the city of Portland, then the state of Oregon, then the Pacific Northwest, later California, and, finally, expansion into the United States and then to Europe.

But it could have been otherwise, being the decision on strategy always important as it determines the level of demand (a function of the climate, culture, and purchasing power) and the level of competition.[93]

Another example of the importance of the choice of the geographical areas is given by **Getir's** acquisition of **Gorillas** in December 2022. The theory of business of both companies was the same: *fast delivery of grocery products.*

But *Gorillas*, cash-starved, was acquired after only 2.5 years of its inception by *Getir*, which, although, having started earlier, is still in operation. This was in great part due to its choice of different geographical areas, such as Turkey, where Getir is quite profitable.

And internationalization also played a role in the turnaround of **Spotify**: from losses of around half a billion in 2022 and 2023, to profits of over 1.1 billion in 2024.

Podcasts offer was aggressively expanded into new markets, as well as *audiobooks* in ever more languages: French, Dutch, and German.

The *AI playlist feature*, which allows users to create playlists through text prompts (set of instructions by AI) initially launched in the UK and Australia in April 2024, was soon also available in the United States, Canada, Ireland, and New Zealand.

The *daylist playlist*, a personalized playlist, that evolves throughout the day based on listener's habits, has been, after English, in a rollout for additional languages: Arabic, French, German, Japanese, and Spanish.

Then from Spotify's expanded audience network followed the new *advertising* markets, in India, Japan, Brazil, or Mexico.

---

[93]Given the *death of distance* (improvement in communications, transportation) and *trade liberalization,* the choice of geographical area can be more or less relevant depending upon the type of goods. Sometimes, geography impacts on marketing operations and logistics. Other times, especially when goods are intangible, it does not.

And continuing to prioritize language location and a commitment to connecting with small markets users, Spotify has added Basque, Galician, and Catalan languages, with the latter strengthening its partnership with FC Barcelona fans.

Then *besides geography*, strategy also involves the choice of **the segment**, which sometimes is defined, that is predetermined by the theory of business (e.g., in the case of Nike above), other times not.

But it is nevertheless always important. Elon Musk's **Tesla** and Shai Agassi's **Better Place** had the same theory of business for electric cars. But their choice of models (segments within a given geographical area) determined their fate.

Both started with *sedans*,[94] but while that segment was appropriate for the U.S. market (and thus for Tesla), that was not the case with Better Place, which should have chosen a subcompact (a very small car) for the Israeli market: *Tel Aviv* being the richest part of Israel is also the *fifth* most traffic-congested city in the world.

And then both companies illustrate again the importance of the choice of the *geographical area*.

Tesla started in Silicon Valley where the acquisition of an electric car was a status symbol: a statement that the buyer cared for the environment; Shai Agassi's Better Place, however, did not pursue its initial huge success in Tokyo, in the taxis niche.

In short, a theory of business *always* determines the **industry**. And *sometimes* it does the same for **segments**. But *rarely* so for the **geographical**

---

[94]The very first car of Tesla was not a sedan but a sports car named Roadster. However, it was never mass-produced, acting more as a test bed for Tesla sedan (the S model) to learn about electric vehicles production, battery technology, and market demand: The technology in the original Roadster was quite nascent compared to Tesla's S sedan with its important advancements in powertrains, battery technology, and manufacturing processes.

areas: The exceptions are products with close links to local culture as the cases of the Turkish Cola and Mecca Cola, that focus respectively on Turkey and the Muslim world, where they aim to create a direct substitute to both Coke and Pepsi.

Here, the theory of business predetermines all three elements of strategy, namely the geographic area (the Muslim world), the industry (soft drinks), and the segment (colas).

Table 6 summarizes the relationship between the theory of business and strategy, that is the degree to which the former predetermines the latter varies.

In any case, **whatever is not predetermined by the theory of business** (on segment, and/or geography) **requires well-thought**, sound, strategic decisions—independent of the theory of business.[95]

But then, just as *strategy* follows (at least in part) from the *theory of business*, the same happens regarding the **tactics and the business model**, with the former implementing the latter.

Table 6 The degree to which the theory of business predetermines strategy

Theory of business Predetermines	Strategy		
Examples	Geographical area	Industry	Segment
Nike	No	Yes	Yes
Tesla	No	Yes	No
Better Place	No	Yes	No
Spotify	No	Yes	Yes
Turkish Cola	Yes	Yes	Yes
Mecca Cola	Yes	Yes	Yes

[95] The general criteria to select the strategy are: (1) attractiveness (sales volume, growth, and margin), (2) competitive advantage, and (3) synergy. And all the three apply to the choice of (A) geographical areas, (B) industries, and (C) segments. Alike.

For instance, **Spotify's** *business model* is characterized by (1) the absence of a *platform* (contrary to Apple Music and YouTube Music), (2) the existence of *two pillars* (of free and premium options, and not only the latter as with Napster), and (3) how they interrelate (the advantages of the premium over the free option).

But then there is still—it remains open—the issue of how each pillar operates, and that is the realm of **tactics**: the marketing, the human resources, the contracts with suppliers—all the **nine functional areas** in Figure 35, of Page 128, before.

These must be periodically reviewed to ensure that actions did not drift away from established policies; due to environmental changes; and because of benchmarks that may appear.

And that pertains to all areas of *tactics*, to all *functional areas*, for instance, **human resources**.

For starts to put on check the *growth of staff*, as exemplified by *Farfetch* and *Gorillas* performing several recent downsizings; *Marks & Spencer* (the UK department store for the middle and middle-upper classes offering home goods, clothes and food) cutting across the board 20 percent of its corporate employees; and *Spotify* laying off 25 percent of its personnel in 2023 (as it had 3 times lower productivity than Netflix in terms of gross margin per employee).

Still in the area of human resources, to achieve its turnaround, *Marks & Spencer standardized working hours* abandoning a far too complex previous system, made *wage increases* dependent on quality of service and not length of time with the company, and improved *customer service* by having the entire store workforce of 56,000 people going through motivational training sessions (sometimes 5,000 employees at a time).

Financial policies can also make a difference. Contrary to *Tesla*, Agassi's company *Better Place* did not benefit either from large *pre-payments* from clients or *government*-supported loans and tax credits or financial markets' support through *IPOs* (initial public offerings).

And it can also be recalled that the example of Marks & Spencer in the previous chapter illustrated the importance of tactical/functional policies in other areas.

Operations were fundamental for *Marks & Spencer* recovery, as it implemented several tactical policies to decrease the *cost of stock* which had reached 3 billion pounds (35 weeks of sales). Among them: *centralizing* the hierarchy levels at which orders were made, creating a *top management job specialized* in inventory control, *weekly meetings* with the CEO participation, and *re-centering the inventory* on core products.

Then also in **logistics** Marks & Spencer *opened five sourcing offices* (Hong Kong, India, Bangladesh, Turkey, and Sri Lanka) to concentrate subcontracting and decrease transportation costs among manufacturers of the several parts of the final product.

Marketing was another area where Marks & Spencer acted upon: on *merchandising*, with a major program of store-by-store refurbishment to make them less dark, cluttered, and blend; on *advertising*, refocusing on food and not clothes or home goods; and in *pricing*, creating three options for every product: good, better, and best.

And naturally, several **functional policies/tactics** are *interrelated*, as some impact on other(s): one of the reasons that led to the demise of Gorillas is that growing too fast, it created too many dark stores (warehouses to supply clients) in a very short period and thus burned cash (finance area) at the rate of $60 million per month.

Figure 36 uses the case of **Marks & Spencer** to illustrate the *relationship* between the *business model* (as discussed in Section 5.1.2 of the previous chapter) and *tactics* (under the new CEO Leo Stuart Rose).

Business model (from page 103)		Examples of tactics (under CEO Stuart Rose)	
A—Assuming total initiative and control of	Product design	Logistics	Opening of five sourcing offices (in Hong Kong, India, Bangladesh, Turkey, and Sri Lanka) to concentrate subcontracting and decrease transportation costs
	Developing the prototypes	Supply chain	Restructuring with suppliers help to decrease costs in 100 million
	Finding the best factories	Control (of stock)	Creation of a top management function exclusively to control inventory and reporting directly to the CEO
			Rule of weekly meetings with the CEO's presence
			Various supporting teams to supply information
B—With a decentralized decision making process	Close to the clients	Human resources	Standardization of working hours
			Wage increases dependent on quality of service
			Improving customer service with training sessions
			20% layoffs of corporate employees
		Marketing — Pricing	Three price options for every product: good, better, best
		Merchandising	Major store-by-store refurbishment
		Advertising	Refocus on food (and not clothes and home goods)

Figure 36 Marks & Spencer business model and tactics

It can thus be said that the difference between the business model and tactics is twofold:

- First, tactics **implement** the business model (and the strategy as per Figure 1 in Page 3); and
- Second (and consequently), it is also a question of **detail**. Tactics are the fine print of the business model. And so they differ in number. While tactics are in the dozens, the business model has only three or four pillars, at most.

Tactics involve innumerous policies related to the *nine functional areas*: marketing, finance, accounting, operations, human resources, administration (general maintenance, hygiene, etc.), information systems, general management (organization chart, control, and coordination mechanisms), and R&D.

The business model, by opposition, constitutes just a few *stepping stones* the internal organization of the company is built upon, and the *basic pillars* capture the essential of how the company works.

The (initial) business model for **Dollar Shave Club** was:

1. Monthly *home delivery* of
2. Grooming products *imported* from South Korea;
3. Under *several subscription plans.*

Of **SpaceX**?:

1. *Renewable* rockets;
2. Mostly done *internally* (vertical integration); and
3. When outsourced using or adapting as need be already *existing* components (not creating anew to reduce costs).

Nike (at the very start)?: Simply

1. *All* production outsourced to a *single* manufacturer: Onitsuka factory in Japan; and
2. *Direct selling* at (1) sports and (2) industry (fairs) events in Oregon state.

But then, of course, one makes the way as one moves along, and as circumstances change, the business model must be adapted.

In the case of Nike, when Japan became too expensive, it was replaced by South Korea, and, within marketing, promotion came to rely increasingly on sponsorships of athletes (Michael Jordan, etc.), and sales became indirect through independent chains.

If a policy is **paramount, fundamental**, to describe how the company operates (and as said for every business, there are **only** a few of them), then it is a **pillar** of the organization and part of the **business model**. And for every business, there are no more than three or four of such stepping stones.

The **other dozens of policies belong to tactics**. They implement the business model, and they **detail the organizational functioning.** But they are far from being irrelevant. After all, frequently it is the small things that make a great difference. It is only that they are not structural.

And they must be periodically **reviewed.** Just as previous chapters went over the steps to follow in the cases of the *theory of business*, the *strategy*, and the *business model*, there are also **four tools** frequently useful to **update tactics.**

They are:

- Benchmarking;
- The *future which already happened*;
- *Planned abandonment*; and
- *Sensitivity analysis*.

The next section (before concluding) will address their use with **Spotify**.

6.4. Spotify: Exemplifying Tools to Upgrade Tactics

Figure 37 schematizes the *relationship* between *tools* and *tactical actions*.

Spotify: the impact of tools on tactics

Actions		Tools	Bench marking	Future which already happened	Planned abandonment	Sensitivity analysis	Internal brain-storming
M A R K E T I N G	New products	Video podcasts	✓				
		Karaoke	✓				
		Audiobooks	✓				
		Music videos	✓				
		Savings in promotion				✓	
		One to one marketing				✓	✓
Human resources		Layoffs	✓				
Opera tions		Owning the content	✓				
		Change in royalties agreements				✓	
		Exclusive agreements with top performers					✓
Underperforming podcasts					✓		
Artificial intelligence				✓			

Figure 37 Spotify: The impact of tools on tactics

The columns list the tools starting with benchmarking. And the lines indicate their impact, on the introduction of karaoke, audiobooks, and so on.

And within cells the ☑ mark indicates which tools generated which initiatives.

Starting with benchmarking, best if done with **(1) top performing (2) direct competitors**, it led Spotify to introduce video podcasts (in 6/2020), karaoke (6/2022), audiobooks (9/2022), and music videos (3/2024), all after Apple had already done so through **Apple Music** or other related platforms.

Next, it may be also fruitful to look at **successful indirect competitors**, such as **Netflix,** which are in the same industry (streaming) but in a different segment (movies, not music).

Having started the streaming service in 2007, Netflix lost money only in the first five years (from 1998 to 2002) and has since then been consistently profitable and ever more so: reaching the mark of $1 billion in 2018, then increased to over $5 billion last year.

The first major difference regarding Spotify is that Netflix *owns the content*: regardless if it is internally developed or acquired. Thus, no royalties are due with every stream as happens with Spotify (and regardless if the subscribers opt for the premium or free alternatives).[96]

Thus, starting in 2019, Spotify invested heavily in acquiring firms such as Gimlet Media, Anchor, and Parcast, which allowed it to produce and host exclusive podcast content.

Then Netflix also outperformed Spotify with three times its productivity in terms of gross margin per *employee*.

---

[96]There are other minor differences such as Netflix offering within the paying option a cheaper plan that includes ads.

And so Spotify laid off 25 percent of its staff in 2023, all part of *"substantial action to right size costs,"* in the words of CEO Daniel Ek.

While Figure 37 indicates only the differences between Spotify and **best direct** (*Apple*) and **indirect** (*Netflix*) competitors, benchmarking can be extended to **other types of competition.**

It is so that Figure 38 indicates that *Tidal* and *Amazon Music* offer lossless audio, and Amazon Music also offers livestreams, that is, real-time videos that are sent over the Internet without any previous recording and storage.

FEATURES OFFERED BY OTHER TYPE OF COMPETITORS THAT SPOTIFY DOES NOT	
Tidal	Lossless audio (top quality + etc.)
Amazon music	Lossless audio (top quality + etc.)
	Livestreams (real time videos sent over the internet without being previously recorded and stored)
Napster	Lossless audio (top quality + etc.)
	Car mode feature
Miao	Direct interaction with stars

Figure 38 Features offered by other type of competitors that Spotify does not

Napster provides lossless audio and a car-mode feature that facilitates navigation when the user is driving.

And *Miao*, a Chinese platform, allows for interaction with stars, such as actors, singers, and influencers, through live chats. Customers are charged by the second and fans can enter a kind of "stock market" to trade with other clients the seconds they have bought.

Naturally, not all initiatives suggested by benchmarking should be followed.

In **Peter Drucker's** words, some are opportunities, others distractions, depending on their difference in terms of (1) *value*, (2) *technical feasibility*, and (3) *cost*, which can be evaluated by (A) *external reports*, (B) insights from the *marketing staff*, (C) the *engineering* department, and (D) the *finance/accounting* department, the latter being the best equipped to consider all types of costs, not only *direct*, but also *indirect* and to seek rather than the technical, the best optimum (Figure 39).

Criteria Information sources	1 Value	2 Technical feasibility	3 Cost
A　External reports	✓		
B　Marketing staff	✓		
C　Engineering department		✓	
D　Finance/ Accounting			✓

Figure 39　Selecting the best opportunities

And the best options would be those whose sums of the three rankings of value, cost, and technical feasibility are lowest.

The hypothetical example of Figure 40 is that the best valence is lossless audio (overall sum of the rankings of five), then livestreams (sum of seven), followed by car mode (10), and so on, with **focus** requiring the sequential offer of the features with the lowest total sum (right-side column).

SELECTING THE BEST FEATURES OFFERED BY COMPETITORS				
Features	Ranking value	Ranking technical feasibility	Ranking lower cost	Sum
Lossless audio	1st	2nd	2nd	5th
Livestreams	2nd	4th	1st	7th
Car mode	4th	3rd	3rd	10th
Etc.	Etc.	Etc.	Etc.	Etc.

Figure 40 Selecting the best features offered by competitors

The *second* and *third* tools to update tactics (in Figure 37 of Page 139) were both suggested by *Peter Drucker*,[97] founder of modern management and they are:

- "*The future which has already happened*," and
- *Planned abandonment.*

The **future which has already happened** is basically rather than making predictions (difficult since it is far easier to create the future than to predict it), to look at the present to identify what is about to boom, to explode. The present that is "pregnant" with the future.

Thus, instead of future trends, one must focus on the futurity of present trends—and what they mean for one's business and the opportunities they create.

In short, one is looking for events that **have already occurred** but whose main and full impact is **yet to come**.

In the last few years one of such events is **artificial intelligence**.[98]

---

[97]Drucker (1995).

[98]A new technology, if major, can have multiple uses, thus enabling improvements in more than one competitiveness driver. It is so that **AI** which enabled to better the *business model* of Spotify can also play a role in upgrading *tactics*. In both. Given its importance.

A few statistics make the point. AI investments surged from $18 billion in 2014 to $119 billion in 2021. And by 2023, AI accounted for around 30 percent of all investments.

The global AI market of $195 billion in 2023 is expected to double by 2025 with AI predicted to generate $15.7 trillion in additional revenue to the global economy by 2030, boosting global GDP by 26 percent.

While naturally adoption varies across industries, it is greatest in information and communication (near 30 percent) as exemplified by ChatGPT that gained over 100 million users in two months.

Spotify invested heavily in AI. Starting a decade ago with the acquisition of Seed Scientific, followed by Niland in 2017 and the expansion of the partnership with Google Cloud in 2024.

The resulting recent benefits include in 2023 *AI DJ* (that curates playlists to listeners recent habits) and in 2024 *AI playlists* (allowing users to create playlists based on text prompts), *Daylist* (a daily mix tailored to different times of the day), the *AI podcast* (which offers personalized comments on listeners habits), and the *remix feature* (a tool that allows users to edit and blend tracks within Spotify).

And so, as a consequence of Gustav Söderström's (co-president and CTO) emphasis on the importance of AI in shaping the future of music streaming, Spotify obtained a competitive edge in both personalization and interactivity.

The other Peter Drucker's tool to upgrade tactics deals not with creating the future but with the absolute reverse, abandoning the past and doing that in a systematic, planned, way: **planned abandonment.**

It is based on a simple question: *If we were to decide now, would we still have the same policies/programs we have today? And if not, what are we going to do about that?*

Indeed, since the world changes every day, no one can afford the luxury of copying the past. And, therefore, the once-relevant policies and projects become obsolete with time, requiring to periodically "clean the locker room." Whatever is in there, left untouched, never commits suicide.

Peter Drucker's recommendation of planned abandonment, which is a re-birth of the ancient Roman practice of **sunset rules: what is admitted for a period will be refused after that period** (ad tempus concessa post tempus censatur de negate); its objective is to reduce servitude to the past, by peri-odically putting all tactical policies, programs, and projects on trial for their lives. And with the burden of proof on their usefulness. Not the contrary.

Since nothing is immortal and the useless weakens the necessary, the ques-tion is: What do I have to abandon today to create room for tomorrow? Before asking ourselves if we are doing things right, we should ask if we are doing the right things. *First things first, second things never* (Peter Drucker).

And so planned abandonment is like trimming a tree so that it can grow. In the words of J. K. Rowling (Harry Potter's creator): *It is our choices, far more than our abilities which show what we truly are.*

When Steve Jobs after being ousted rejoined **Apple,** he found 350 ongo-ing projects. He terminated all except 10 and the resulting focus enabled Apple to revolutionize **three** industries: *information systems* (with PCs), *music* (with iPod and iTunes), and *communications* (with smartphones).

And in recent years, **Spotify** practiced planned abandonment in **three** major areas:

First, **products**. The *Car Thing* was Spotify's first hardware product: a device to enhance in-car audio streaming experiences. Launched in 2022, it was discontinued in December 2024 because of low demand with the company citing its decision to abandon hardware ventures to focus on improving its services. This is a good example for the principle that *the first step to grow is to decide what to withdraw from.*

Second, the same principle was applied to **several service offers**, such as the *Music + Talk*,[99] which allowed to combine music tracks with spoken commentary. Its unique format assured that there was no competition in the target niche.

But there was neither demand. And so it was discontinued in June 2024.

And a **third** major area was *podcasts*. Introduced in 2015, only recently was it transformed from a continuous loss (a "drag until 2023" in CEO Daniel Ek's words), into a profit center.

True, it was achieved by several policies besides planned abandonment, such as greater *personalization* with the use of AI to better match listeners with podcasts; *multiyear partnerships* of top-performing podcasts (such as the Joe Rogan experience signed in February 2024); the *acquisition* of the companies Gimlet Media, Anchor, and Parcast to produce content; and the introduction of *innovations* such as video podcasts.

But also through **planned abandonment** of all underperformers, even if signed with celebrities (such as Harry and Meghan) and regardless if high investments had already been done ($25 million in the Duke and Duchess case). All underperforming and low-impact shows were cut in order to focus on high-return projects.

Thus, the above actions by Spotify are a good example of accepting sunk costs, rather than through rationalization projecting past losses into the future.

Finally, a **fourth** frequently useful tool in drawing tactical plans is **sensitivity analysis**, which involves several steps:

First, making an income, or cash-flow *statement*;

---

[99]As many other service features: Type Script API, WebAPI Node, certain API Endpoints, and so on.

Second, *detailing* it to the level of 15/20 variables;

Third, asking *what if questions*: What will happen to the bottom line (percentage of change), if 1 percent of each item/line in the income or cash-flow statement would change? Is it the price, or frequency of purchase, costs of packaging, or of a certain component, or in transportation, warehousing direct labor, and so on? Or is it the machinery capacity utilization? Corporate labor costs? Back-office costs? Or administrative costs (maintenance, hygiene, security)? All of these can be pertinent.

Fourth, after asserting how sensitive the bottom line (profits or cash) is to percentual changes in each variable and in order to narrow down where to act upon, it is useful to *deepen the analysis by subdividing that variable* in its various components; for instance, distinguishing among the various types of direct labor or back-office costs.

And **fifth:** One stops the above process when the *impact* on the bottom line starts diminishing significantly (decreasing returns).

The **two** great advantages of sensitivity analysis is that it yields information regarding (1) where *controls* are most *needed* (the items to which the bottom line is most sensitive to) and (2) where to *act now in* order to improve performance.

Should **Spotify** drop some (or all) of the 20 percent of the songs list which are never played? Or increase the frequency of ads in the free option (at present one ad every three songs)? Or act upon the clause of minimum level of payment in the royalties contracts? Or change the contracts royalties from fixed to variable according to how many times each song is played? Or change the ads prices? Or decrease headcounts? Or limits the hours of free users? Or...?

As a matter of fact, Spotify's royalties contracts with suppliers had **three** major drawbacks.

First, royalties were due *every time* free-option users played a song. Since ads did not cover royalties costs, the higher the number of streams, the greater the losses.

Second, contracts stipulated *minimums* to be paid.

And *third*, *20 percent* of the songs were never played (but nevertheless royalties were paid on them).

Thus, although the prices charged by Spotify were only slightly lower than those of the major competitor Apple Music[100], Spotify's gross margin (prices minus variable costs/cost of goods sold) was nearly 2.6 times lower than Apple's.

Consequently, the major cause of Spotify's losses was not price, but the variable costs, and here was where one had to act upon.

So, starting in April 2024, Spotify introduced major changes to its **royalty policies**, among them a *minimum* stream requirement: to be eligible for royalties tracks must achieve a threshold of 1,000 streams/year; improved technology to detect *artificial* streaming; and the requirement that tracks be at least *two* minutes long to qualify for royalties.[101]

Other priority tactical changes suggested by sensitivity analysis were the layoffs of 25 percent of the *workforce* in 2023, since Spotify's productivity per employee in terms of gross margin was three times below that of Netflix.

---

[100]Spotify and Apple prices were the same for the individual, family, and student plans. But Spotify also offered a duo plan (which Apple did not), with prices that made it cheaper per person, if one opted for the duo plan.
[101]To improve its gross margin, in 2024, Spotify also increased prices per month for its individual plan from $10.99 to $11.99 per month, duo plan from $14.99 to $16.99, and family plan from $16.99 to $19.99 (with the student plan remaining at $5.99), thus placing its overall pricing slightly above Apple's.

And significant *savings in marketing* were implemented throughout 2023: cutting paid promotion campaigns and discount, to acquire new users.

Although later CEO Daniel Ek recognizes that *"the company had pulled back too significantly on marketing expenditure,"* many of the savings remained in place since the policy now is a *more targeted* approach to promotion: (1) acquiring and reactivating *high-value users*, (2) achieving *deeper engagement* by the user base, and (3) *partnering* promotions with other brands to co-market its platform.

Spotify's changes in its *royalties* policy, *layoffs*, and *savings in promotion* illustrate the utility of **sensitivity analysis**.

And the fact that layoffs were also a consequence of benchmarking (in Figure 37 of Page 139) exemplifies that a single course of action can be suggested by more than one tool.

Furthermore, the **fast grocery delivery business** indicates that sensitivity analysis is useful *across* a broad range of industries.

Indeed, most companies in the *fast grocery delivery business* lose money. And many left the market: Homegrocer, Peapod, FreshDirect, Frichti, Buyk, Fridge No More, and so on.[102]

So the surviving companies could very well *benefit* from ascertaining the impact on the bottom line with **what if questions** such as: Increase in the minimum value per order? Augment the number of expensive products in each delivery? Change the fixed fee per order? Raise prices? Create several options for time delivery (charging less for slower ones)? Put ads in the sites, bikes, and food bags? Discontinue foods with thinner margins? Renegotiate margins with some suppliers?. And so on.

In short, the value of sensitivity analysis is that it questions previous managerial decisions, made under specific reality assumptions. These

---

[102]In recent years, some exceptions include Gousto, Uber Eats, and Instacart.

sometimes were incorrect. But even when sound in the past, the passage of time made them obsolete.

And so **sensitivity analysis complements the planned abandonment tool**.

The latter frees a company of the *excessive*. The former o*ptimizes* what should remain. All together make for *better performance*.

But *both* focus on getting rid of the **past**. By opposition to the *two other* tools for tactical change (what is the future that has already happened and benchmarking), that directly question the **future**.

Thus, the **four tools** are not only useful by themselves but they complement each other.

And so, although not all tactical changes follow from them, as others can be a consequence of **internal brainstorming** such as Spotify 2024 adhesion to one-to-one marketing by creating a new plan Basic priced below Premium, the **four** techniques can be quite useful to **upgrade tactics**.

6.5. Summing Up

Businesses exist to make a profit. Losses mean taking out from society more (in resources) than what is returned in value (sales). In one word: **destruction**.

Sure that sometimes it takes longer first to achieve the breakeven, then profits, and finally the payback (when at last the sum of profits compensate previous losses).

It is so that **Tesla** achieved profitability only at the 12th year of its existence (2020). **Uber Eats**' EBITDA was negative for five years until 2022. And **Uber**, the whole company, having started in 2009, collected losses (with the single exception of 2018) year after year, until finally in 2023 its bottom line was positive. Furthermore, **Spotify** for 18 consecutive years (2006–2023) accumulated losses until it finally achieved 1.1 billion euros profit in 2024.

But companies should expect to give *money* back to its shareholders and not require endless *patience* from them. The longer the series of losses, the greater the risk of the firm's demise.

And the above holds true regardless of the market value a company is able to achieve, even if it is a unicorn. That much is illustrated by the **disappearance** of *Gorillas, Farfetch, Homegrocer, Buyk, Fridge No More, Grubhub,* and so many others. All of these are unicorns. And all of these have gone.

To avoid such mishaps and in order to be **competitive**, a firm must have **four sound, well-designed, drivers**: (1) a *theory of business* (the why), (2) *strategy* (the where), (3) *business model* (the what), <u>and</u> (4) *tactics* (the how).

The four are distinct. All are **necessary**, neither sufficient by itself for optimizing performance. And they **interrelate** as per Figure 34 in Page 127.

It all starts with a **theory of business,** which is a set of *assumptions* about reality the organization is built upon. Why it makes sense.

In the case of **Warby Parker** (a unicorn built upon home delivery of glasses) they are: (1) in-store buying is far too *expensive* and (2) the *net* now allows for customers to virtually *try* glasses.

Here the *industry* (eyewear), which is one of the three areas of **strategy**, comes *predetermined* by the theory of business, but two other components of strategy *do not*.

First, the *segment* within the eyewear industry remains *open to choice*: Should it be prescription or sunglasses or both? The price level (thus, the quality of the frames and lens[103])? For men or women? Only glasses or also contact lenses? How broad are the uses (segments) covered: including special-purpose glasses for sports and hobbies, as well as other optic instruments? And so on.

And then comes the choice of the *geographical areas* of operations, which *remains to be decided upon*, depending on trade barriers, logistics (and thus delivery time), level of competition, and the cost of off-net (and thus local) promotion.

So these two aspects of strategy, the selection of the *segment* and *geographical areas*, remain **independent** of the business theory. But they are equally relevant for success. And being important, there is **freedom of choice**, not predetermination.

Then the **business model** regards the main pillars, the stepping stones of the company's **organization**. And again in the case of **Warby Parker** they are three: (1) the quality of the *digital application* which allows customers using the net to simulate in-store trying of glasses, (2) to decrease the purchase risk both through customer-friendly technical specifications and a money-back guarantee policy, and (3) a fast and safe delivery process.

And finally from both the strategy and business model follow the **tactics**: choosing the suppliers, logistics, finance, cost control, product design, the cost accounting system, human resources policies, promotion, and so on (all functional areas previously listed in Figure 34 of Page 127).

Nike's first attempt at advertising was a handout designed and produced at a local print shop that read: "*Best news in flats! Japan challenges European track shoe domination! Low Japanese labor costs make it possible for an exciting new firm to offer these shoes at the low, low price of $6.95.*" At the bottom was the address and phone number.

---

[103]Prices vary extremely from the low end of Pentax or Kodak (brand recognition but limited innovation), to the top of Zeiss (the pinnacle of lens innovation) or Nikon (the most expensive brand in the world).

Thus, there are **four wheels** for an organization's competitiveness. Failure in one affects overall performance. And so an organization must be seen as a **car**, *not a two- or three-wheeled vehicle.*[104]

If one of the four competitiveness drivers is neglected, the most a company can hope to achieve is **efficiency** (*doing things right*), but not **effectiveness** (*doing the right things*).

With the consequence that, at least in part, company efforts will be **off target**. With more and more actions producing less and less results. Ever-decreasing returns. All culminating by *doing well the (almost) irrelevant*.

Therefore, the need to recognize that **business performance has four drivers**. And to act upon all four *simultaneously*, not on part of them.

---

[104]Most brands from Harley Davison to Morgan and including Gilera, Kymco, Piaggio, Polaris, and so on besides two-wheel motorcycles also have three-wheel motorcycles.

Selected References

This book is mostly based on *primary research* (data directly collected from original sources) which was first used to publish academic articles on the book's material.

But then also on *secondary research*, namely some major works that were quoted along the text in footnotes.

On the latter, it may nevertheless be useful to list all of them together, be they books or articles. So, by alphabetic order they are:

Aagaard, A. 2024. *Business Model Innovation: Game Changers and Contemporary Issues*. Palgrave Macmillan.

Ademi, B., N. J. Klungseth, and N. O. E. Olsson. 2021. "Strategic Flexibility and Business Model Innovation: A Literature Review." Paper presented at the *European Academy of Management (EURAM) 2021 Conference—Reshaping Capitalism for a Sustainable World,* June 16–18, 2021.

Bellman, R., C. Clark, C. Craft, D. Malcolm, and F. Ricciardi. 1957. "On the Construction of a Multi-Stage, Multi-Person Business Game." *Operations Research* 5: 469–503.

Bigelow, L. S., and J. B. Barney. 2021. "What can Strategy Learn from the Business Model Approach?" *Journal of Management Studies* 58: 528–39.

Booth, B. 2019. "What Happens When a Business Built on Simplicity Gets Complicated? Dollar Shave Club's founder Michael Dubin Found Out." *CNBC*, March 24, 2019. https://www.cnbc.com/2019/03/23/dollar-shaves-dubin-admits-a-business-built-on-simplicity-can-get-complicated.html.

Borgonovo, E. 2017. *Sensitivity Analysis: An Introduction for the Management Scientist*. Springer.

Bradshaw, T. 2022. "Most Rapid Grocery Apps Fail to Deliver for Investors." *Financial Times*, October 14, 2022. https://www.ft.com/content/be07c7ae-765d-4d29-b8cd-26ad8b4ccaed.

Carroll, P. 1994. *Big Blues. The Unmaking of IBM*. Three Rivers Press.

Casadesus-Masanell, R., and J. E. Ricart. 2011. "How to Design a Winning Business Model." *Harvard Business Review* 89 (1–2): 100–7.

Christensen, C. 1997. *The Innovator's Dilemma: When New Technologies Cause Great Firms to Fail*. Harvard Business Review Press.

DaSilva, C. M., and P. Trkman. 2014. "Business Model: What It Is and What It Is Not." *Long Range Planning* 47 (6): 379–89.

Dean, B. 2024. "Spotify User Stats." *Backlinko*, April 4, 2024. https://backlinko.com/spotify-users.

De Villiers Scheepers, M. J., S. Gronum, S. Cranney, and N. Tracey. 2024. "Business Model Redesign Through Effectual Action in Times of Crisis." *Journal of Small Business Management* 1–37.

Drucker, P. F. 1973. *Management*. 1st ed. Harper & Row. Reprint, 2008. Harper Business.

Drucker, P. F. 1992. *Managing for the Future: The 1990s and Beyond*. Truman Talley Books.

Drucker, P. F. 1994. "The Theory of the Business." *Harvard Business Review*, September–October, 1994. https://hbr.org/1994/09/the-theory-of-the-business.

Drucker, P. F. 1995. *Innovation and Entrepreneurship*. Butterworth–Heinemann.

Drucker, P. F. 2008. *The Essential Drucker: The Best of Sixty Years of Peter Drucker's Essential Writings on Management*. Collins Business Essentials. *Harper Business*.

Drucker, P. F., J. Collins, P. Kotler, et al. 2008. *The Five Most Important Questions You Will Ever Ask About Your Organization*. Jossey-Bass.

Drucker, P. F., and N. Stone. 2003. "On the Profession of Management." In *Harvard Business Review Book*, edited and introduction by Nan Stone. Harvard Business School Publishing.

Dvir, D., and O. Emet. 2016. "Better Place—Revolutionary Idea: The Vision and Reality." *Coller School of Management, Tel Aviv University*, November, 2016.

Essbaa, E., S. Laraqui, and B. Jarreau. 2025. "Adapting Global Business Models to Disruptive Innovation and Market Dynamics: A Framework for Modern Times." *The Journal of Organizational Management Studies* 2025.

Gassmann, O., M. Csik, and K. Frankenberger. 2014. *The Business Model Navigator: 55 Models That Will Revolutionise Your Business*. FT Press.

Gerstner Jr., L. V. 2002. *Who Says Elephants Can't Dance? Inside IBM's Historic Turnaround*. Harper Business.

Isaacson, W. 2023. *Elon Musk*. Simon & Schuster.

Johnson, M. W., C. M. Christensen, and H. Kagermann. 2008. "Reinventing your business model." *Harvard Business Review* 86 (12): 50–9.

Knight, P. 2016. *Shoe Dog: A Memoir by the Creator of Nike*. Simon & Schuster.

Koprivnjak, T., and S. Oberman Peterka. 2020. "Business Model as a Base for Building Firms' Competitiveness." *Sustainability* 12 (21): 9278.

Kotler, P. 2017. *My Adventures in Marketing: The Autobiography of Philip Kotler*. Idea Bite Press.

Kroc, R. 1977. *Grinding It Out: The Making of McDonald's*. St. Martin's Publishing.

Löfsten, H., A. Isaksson, H. Rannikko, E. Tornikoski, and M. Buffart. 2025. "Impact of Initial Business Model on the Growth Trajectory of New Technology-Based Firms: A Path Dependency Perspective." *Journal of Technology Transfer* 50: 29–61.

Love, J. F. 1987. *McDonald's: Behind the Arches*. Bantam Books.

Magretta, J. 2002. "Why Business Models Matter." *Harvard Business Review* 80: 86–92.

Maucuer, R., and A. Renaud. 2019. "Business Model Research: A Bibliometric Analysis of Origins and Trends." *M@n@gement* 22.

McGrath, R. G., and S. Cliffe. 2011. "When Your Business Model Is in Trouble." *Harvard Business Review*, January–February 2011. https://hbr.org/2011/01/when-your-business-model-is-in-trouble.

Meghalaroia. 2022. "The Dollar Shave Club: An Extraordinary Story of an Ordinary Product Brand." *Velocity Blog*, March 9, 2022. https://blog.velocity.in/the-dollar-shave-club-an-extraordinary-story-of-an-ordinary-product-brand/.

Meyersohn, N. 2021. "This Company Wants to Deliver Your Groceries in 10 Minutes." *CNN Business*, May 25, 2021. https://edition.cnn.com/2021/05/25/business/gorillas-grocery-delivery-new-york/index.html.

Mills, D. Q. 1996. "The Decline and Rise of IBM." *Sloan Management Review* 37 (4): 78–82.

O'Grady, J. D. 2008. *Apple Inc. (Corporations That Changed the World)*. Greenwood.

Osterwalder, A., and Y. Pigneur. 2010. *Business Model Generation*. John Wiley and Sons.

Osterwalder, A., Y. Pigneur, A. Smith, and F. Etiemble. 2020. *The Invincible Company: How to Constantly Reinvent Your Organization with Inspiration from the World's Best Business Models*. Wiley.

Ovans, A. 2015. "What Is a Business Model?" *Harvard Business Review*, January 23, 2015. https://hbr.org/2015/01/what-is-a-business-model.

Partington, M., and A. Lewin. 2021. "On-Demand Grocery Delivery Startup Gorillas Raises €245m and Becomes a Unicorn, Nine Months After Launch." *Sifted*, March 25, 2021. https://sifted.eu/articles/gorillas-raises-e245m-unicorn.

Peric, M., J. Durkin, and V. Vitezic. 2017. "The Constructs of a Business Model Redefined: A Half-Century Journey." *SAGE Open* 7 (3).

Porter, M. E. 2001. "The Value Chain and Competitive Advantage." *Understanding Business: Processes* 2: 50–66.

Rose, S. 2007, May. "Back in Fashion: How We're Reviving a British Icon." *Harvard Business Review*, May, 2007. https://hbr.org/2007/05/back-in-fashion-how-were-reviving-a-british-icon

Sá, J. V. 1999. *The War Lords: Measuring Strategy and Tactics for Competitive Advantage in Business*. Kogan Page.

Sá, J. V. 2002. *The Neglected Firm*. Palgrave/MacMillan.

Sá, J. V. 2005. *Strategy Moves: 14 Complete Attack and Defence Strategies for Competitive Advantage*. Prentice-Hall/Financial Times.

Sá, J. V. 2015. *Anergy: A Step by Step Approach to Avoid 2+2=3 for Multibusiness Corporations.* Promoculture Larcier.

Sá, J. V., and M. Pereira. 2009. *Drucker on Carving Success Out of the Crisis: What Peter Drucker Would Have Told Us.* Vida Económica.

Saltelli, A., S. Tarantola, F. Campolongo, and M. Ratto. 2004. *Sensitivity Analysis in Practice: A Guide to Assessing Scientific Models.* John Wiley & Sons.

Simpson, M. 2015. *Disruptive Innovation: 12 Game Changing Principles for Marketplace Leaders in The Kingdom Economy.* Xulon Press.

Smith, D. 2013. *How to Think Like Steve Jobs.* Michael O'Mara Books Ltd.

Snihur, Y., and K. M. Eisenhardt. 2022. "Looking Forward, Looking Back: Strategic Organization and the Business Model Concept." *Strategic Organization* 20 (4): 757–70.

Ulwick, A. W. 2016. *Jobs to be Done: Theory to Practice.* Idea Bite Press.

Vance, A. 2015. *Elon Musk—How the Billionaire CEO of SpaceX and Tesla is Shaping our Future.* Penguin Random House.

Van der Pijl, P., J. Lokitz, R. Wijnen, and M. Van Lieshout. 2020. *Business Model Shifts: Six Ways to Create New Value for Customers.* Wiley.

Vatankhah, S., V. Bamshad, L. Altinay, and G. De Vita. 2023. "Understanding Business Model Development Through the Lens of Complexity Theory: Enablers and Barriers." *Journal of Business Research* 155 (Part A).

About the Authors

Jorge Sá

1. Jorge Sá is an expert on Peter Drucker and Philip Kotler, founders of modern management and modern marketing, respectively, who offered letters of recommendation for his books and endorsements for his work.

2. Has a **master's degree** from the Peter F. Drucker Graduate School of Management in California and a **doctorate (PhD)** in Business Administration, from Columbia University, in New York, where he was research, teaching assistant, and graduated with honors (always Dean's list, Beta Gamma Sigma). Also holds a *graduate degree* in Macroeconomics.

3. Was awarded the **Jean Monnet Chair** by the Jean Monnet Foundation, and his **books translated into twelve languages: English, Portuguese, Spanish, Chinese (Mandarin), Russian, Ukrainian, German, Lithuanian, Thai, Korean, Norwegian and Iranian**, received **endorsements**, among others, from Peter F. Drucker, Cecily Drucker, Al Ries (author of the bestsellers Marketing Warfare and Positioning), Don Hambrick (Professor at Columbia University and The Pennsylvania State University), Karl Moore (Professor at Oxford and McGill University), Peter Starbuck (President of the London Drucker Society) and Philip Kotler.

4. Besides **over forty articles published in blind refereed** academic journals (Scopus) on economics, business administration and medicine, he has addressed **conferences and given seminars** at several institutions including TED USA (**https://youtu.be/SOkjPVi1Fts**),

London Business School, Drucker University, IESE, Glasgow Business School, ESSEC (France), ESSAM (European Consortium of Business Schools), Manchester Business School, George Washington University, Oxford, etc. Has also addressed conferences and presented articles in academic and non-academic meetings, such as Academy of Management, Western Economic Association, Peter Drucker Society of Europe, at the European Commission, among others.

5. Has worked as **private consultant, non-executive director** or taught in the **executive programs** of *multinational companies* such as: Coca-Cola, SHELL, Unisys, IBM, Price Waterhouse, KPMG, Glaxo, British Petroleum – BP, Dun & Bradstreet, Deloitte & Touche, Makro (Metro group), Systéme U, I.F.A, Intermarché, Mini Prix Bonjours, Accenture, Watson Wyatt, Cap Gemini, Cesce, Scottish & Newcastle, Sara Lee, Total, Johnson & Johnson, Pfizer, Logica, Indra, Grandvision, Jafep, Euler Hermes, Cosec, Pestana Group Hotels, Tivoli Hotels & Resorts, Millennium Bank, Julius Baer, SGG, Henkel, Abencys, Broadbill, Volkswagen Group, McDonald's, MiTek, United Steel Products, Base Group, United-Health group, Inapa, Vodafone, IDC, Merck, BPI Bank, Milestone, Fijowave, Foxpak, ND Sports, LLR-G5, Horan, Prodieco, Dennison, Grid Finance, Bluemetrix, European Federation of Pharmaceutical Industries and Associations, Microsoft, etc.

6. His **hobbies** are *soccer* (he holds a degree as a professional coach) and *travel* (speaking fluently by alphabetical order English, French, German, Portuguese and Spanish).

Magda Pereira

With an academic background in management has co-authored ten books published in three languages, with topics ranging from business to economics.

On the latter, her latest book (2024) was published by Austin Macauley, London/New York: *Economic Myths and Economic Realities; five mistakes we are told every single day and the real sources of economic growth.*

Index

Absence of a platform, 57
Adidas, 3, 11, 18*n*13, 19, 21, 25
Agassi, Shai, 101
AI playlist feature, 131
Alliance, business model for, 109–112
Amazon, 49, 53–55, 57, 63
Anchor, 140
Apple, 47–51, 53–58, 63, 145
   influence on IBM and PC market,
     80, 86
   vs. Spotify, 114–119
Apple Music, 140
Aristotle, 8
Artificial intelligence, 55–56
ATT, mission accomplished
     example, 80
Audiobooks, 52, 56, 57

Bankruptcy, 110
Best Data, 2, 47
Better Place, 132
Better Place firm
   failure of, 101
Bolt, sales without profit, 105–108
Bowerman, Bill, 11, 14, 16–17, 28
Business model, 46–47, 46*n*37
   definition of, 77, 101
   Dollar Shave Club. *See* Dollar
     Shave Club
   McDonald's. *See* McDonald's
   Nike. *See* Nike
   review process
     for partnerships, 109–112
     for stand-alone firms, 112–120
   review timing, 108–109
   sales without profit, 105–108
   SolarCity, 102
   SolarCity. *See* SolarCity
   SpaceX. *See* SpaceX
   Spotify. *See* Spotify
   strategic shift, 102–105

Tesla and Better Place firm, 102
Business profit formula, 46
Business theory
   evolution of, 76–79
   review process, 82–95
   review timing, 95–97

Canva, 15, 46, 50, 52, 52*n*47, 114–119
   Spotify *vs.*, 54–55
Car Thing, 145
Chanel, 126
Change
   as constant in life, 76
   impact on business assumptions,
     76–79
Chokhmah, 8, 9
Chrysler, 81
Competition, 82–85
Competitiveness drivers, 3, 9. *See also*
     specific drivers
Contract for deed, 68*n*50
Converse, 11, 14, 18, 25
Cortez model, 18
COVID-19 pandemic, 78–79
   Gorillas, case of, 87–90, 95–96
   Sears, case of, 87

Daylist playlist, 131
Decision-making, Marks & Spencer
     case, 103–104
Demand problems, 125
Diamond Multimedia, 47
Dior, 126
Direct to Consumer (DTC)
     marketing, 24–26, 29
Dollar Shave Club, 10, 40–43,
     83–84, 87, 137
   business model, 33
   against Gillette, 31–36
   high price, 31
   home delivery, 31–32

inconvenience, 31
logistics, 34
net promotion, 34
pricing of penetration, 34
product policy, 34
reality assumptions, 32
Schick and, 31–36
strategy, 33
subscription plans, 33–34
tactics, 33–34
theory of business, 31–32, 42
at upstart, 35
Drifting business model, 126
Drucker, Peter, 2, 6, 46n37, 142
Dubin, Michael, 30, 31, 32

Ebit, 51–52, 59
Ebitda, 51n46
Effectiveness, 8–10
Efficiency, 8–10
Ek, Daniel, 49, 55
Entrepreneurial spirit, 66

Farfetch, 124–127
theory of business, 125
Fast grocery delivery business, 149
Faulty business model, performance
and, 48–62
Ford Motor Company, 77
Franchise Realty Corporation,
65, 111
Franchising, McDonald's case,
109–112

General Foods, 65n59
General Motors, segmentation and
unexpected successes, 81–82
Getir, 130
Gillette, 3, 30, 31–36
Gimlet Media, 140
Glovo, sales without profit, 105–108
Gorillas, 131
based on ruptures, 95–96
business model of, 78–79
institutional aspects, 86
sales without profit, 105–108
statistical trends, 87–90
Gousto, 90

IBM
competences for, 77
Gerstner leadership and
transformation, 77–78
reaction to Apple, 80–81
Initial public offering (IPO), 101
Institutional aspects, 86
IOS (iPhone operating system),
57–58
iPod, 47
iTunes, 47

Japan, 19–20, 23–24, 29

Karaoke, 55, 56, 57
Knight, Phil, 11, 13–14, 17, 19–21,
25, 28, 130
Kotler, Philip, 30
Kroc, R., 64, 65–67, 110–111

Lincoln, Abraham, 76–77
Louis Vuitton, 126

Management tools, 55, 56
Marathon, B., 12–13
Marks & Spencer, 134–135
business model and tactics, 136
business model drift case study,
102–105
Marup model, 18
McDonald, 48, 59, 73
business model of, 109–112
characteristics of, 64–65
cleanliness and practicality, 64
control of land, 66
cornerstone of, 63–64
fast service, 63
low prices, 63
quality of food, 64
quality of franchisees, 66
revenues, 66–67
single change, importance of,
63–68
Mecca Cola, 133
Miao, 141
Minute Clinic, 47
Moore's law, 77
Music + Talk, 146

Music videos, 55, 56, 57
Musk, E., 37, 71
Musk, Elon, 101

Napster, 141
Netflix, 140
Nike, 10, 40–43, 130
    Adidas *vs.*, 11
    assumptions, 11–12
    building blocks to, 26
    business plan, 21–30
    comfort, 16, 18, 20
    data and theory testing, 35–87
    direct marketing, 26
    Direct to Consumer marketing,
        24–26, 29
    grip power, 16, 18, 20
    jogging, reasons for increasing,
        13–14
    lightness, 16, 18, 20
    long-term trends, 97–98
    market surveys, 92–95
    Puma *vs.*, 11
    reality assumptions, 90–92
    strategy, 21–22
    tactics, 27–29
    theory of business, 11–21, 40
    at upstart, 27
Nokia, 86

Operations Research, 46

Paramount, fundamental, 138
Parcast, 140
Performance, faulty business model
        and, 48–62
Performance optimization, 100
Phronesis, 8, 9
Podcasts, 52, 56, 131
Porter, M., 2
Profitability, four requirements
        for, 124
Puma, 3, 11, 18, 21, 25

Reality assumptions, 2, 43, 83–86. *See
    also* Theory of business
Reebok, 11, 15, 18*n*13, 25
Rogan, Joe, 146

Rowling, J. K., 145
Royalty policies, 148

S. Bernardino restaurant, 64, 66
Schick, 3, 30, 31–36
Sears Roebuck, theory of business
        realignment, 76–77, 79
Second-hand items, 126
Sensitivity analysis, 146, 148
Söderström, Gustav, 144
SolarCity, 48, 73
    client-perceived risk, 71
    in-house production, 71
    increase of sale, 71
    modifications to sound business
        model, 68–72
    no-money-down policy, 70–71
    profitability, 70–71
    success factors of, 102
    ugliness problem, 71
    upfront investment, 70
Solomon, 8
Sonneborn, Harry, 63, 65, 110
Sound business model, 59. *See also*
        SolarCity
Sound theory of business, 49
SpaceX, 3, 10, 40–43, 83–84
    3 billion people, 36–37
    available consumer electronics, 38
    business model, 37–38, 39
    clients, 37
    low-price rockets, 38
    reality assumptions, 36–37, 42
    small (not truck-sized) satellites, 38
    technology, 37
    theory of business, 36–37, 39–40
    vertical integration, 37–38
Spotify, 48, 72–73, 112, 114, 131
    from 2006 to start of 2022,
        49–50
    access to iPhone users, 57–58
    in artificial intelligence, 55–56
    Canva *vs.*, 54–55
    dismal profitability of, 52
    from early 2022 onwards, 55–59
    free *vs.* premium model analysis,
        119–120
    net income, 50–55

pillars of, 53
strategic changes, 60–62
tactics, 60
turnaround, 52*n*48
upon two fronts, 55
vs. Apple Music and Canva,
    114–119
Stand-alone firms, business model for,
    112–120
Statistical trends, of Gorillas,
    87–90
Strategic mistakes, 101
Strategy, 2, 4, 8–10, 124
    concept of, 128–136
    Dollar Shave Club, 33
    modifications, 52*n*48
    Nike, 21–22

Tactical plans, 2
Tactics, 2, 9, 9*n*6, 21, 23*n*20, 32, 46,
    52, 124
    areas, 2*n*2
    concept of, 128–136
    Dollar Shave Club, 33–34
    exemplifying tools to upgrade,
        138–150
    Nike's, 27–29
    Spotify, 60
    types of, 27, 28
Technical assumptions, 86–87
Tel Aviv, 132

Tesla, 132
    success *vs.* Better Place firm, 101
Theory of business, 2, 6, 46, 124
    business model and, 47
    definition, 76
    Dollar Shave Club, 31–32, 42
    McDonald's. *See* McDonald's
    Nike, 11–21, 40
    review process, 82–95
    review timing, 95–97
    SolarCity. *See* SolarCity
    sound, 49
    SpaceX, 36–37, 39–40
    Spotify. *See* Spotify
    unexpected successes, 80–82
Turkish Cola, 133

Uber, 31*n*26, 32
    sales without profit, 105–108
Unexpected failures, 82
Unexpected successes, 80–82
Unicorn Farfetch, example of,
    124–127

Vehicles industry
    segmentation, 81–82
Vertical integration, 126

Warby Parker, 151–152

YouTube, 49, 53–55, 57

www.ingramcontent.com/pod-product-compliance
Lightning Source LLC
Chambersburg PA
CBHW061314220326
41599CB00026B/4869